FARMING *in the* BLACK PATCH

FARMING *in the* BLACK PATCH

BOBBIE SMITH BRYANT

Acclaim Press
MORLEY, MISSOURI

An old tobacco barn in Calloway County
(Smith family)

Acclaim Press
— Your Next Great Book —

P.O. Box 238
Morley, MO 63767
(573) 472-9800
www.acclaimpress.com

Book & Cover Design: M. Frene Melton
Cover photo: Lynn Bartlett, author of *Tobacco Barns of Western Kentucky*

ISBN: 978-1-942613-06-0 / 1-942613-06-7
Library of Congress Control Number: 2015907827

First Printing: 2015
Printed in the United States of America
10 9 8 7 6 5 4 3 2 1

Contents

Dedication

To my father, Billy Smith.

Daddy is the quiet, behind-the-scenes force that made Farming in the Black Patch *a reality. His love of the land we call home is seeded, watered, and deeply rooted in his children, grandchildren, and great-grandchildren.*

Featured Farms

Carraway Family Farms was founded in 1955 by Noby and Euva Carraway. In 1971, their son and daughter-in-law, Steve and Freda, joined them in the farming operation. In 2006, Noby and Euva's grandson Craig, and his wife, Joanna, purchased their share of the operation and continue to operate the farm today as co-owners with Steve and Freda. Crops raised on the farm include white corn, yellow corn, soybeans, wheat, and canola, along with dark-fired, dark air-cured, and burley tobacco.

When Shea and Scott Lowe married in 2002, they set out to make their dreams come true as farmers. Even though neither of them grew up on a farm, nor had any family members who farmed, they wanted to be first-generation farmers. Since that decision was made, the Lowes have added two daughters to their family, Sayde and Sayler, who are learning all about life on the farm. Today, **Lowe Farms** grows dark tobacco, Angus cattle, corn, soybeans, wheat, and hay.

Smith Farms continues a long heritage of tobacco production, spanning nearly 200 years in Calloway County. In 1982, Billy Dale Smith became owner/operator of Smith Farms, taking over from his dad, William H. Smith, Jr. Today, Billy Dale is helping his son Josh and grandsons, Logan and Carter, as they apply 21st-century techniques to their farming operation. In addition to dark-fired, air-cured and burley tobacco, Smith farms produces corn, soybeans, wheat, and milo.

In 2015, the Marshall County Young Farmers Association recognized **JohnMichael Puckett** with a state award for his dark tobacco production. He continues to grow his farm operation and has now also branched out into row crops, using modern-day equipment necessary to harvest those crops. JohnMichael learned about farming from his father and grandfather and uncle. He has learned a great deal from them and also from observing neighboring farmers.

Danny Cunningham is owner and manager of **Cunningham Farms**, carrying on the farm tradition he learned from his dad and granddad. A hayride and love at first sight eventually led to marriage for Danny and Julia (Judy) Key in 1962. Danny purchased land from his uncle in the Penny community in 1965, and together the Cunninghams raised three daughters. Their oldest, Deana, now helps manage the farm, along with her husband Ricky Chadwick and Elvin Lee Parrish. The operation at Cunningham Farms includes 4,200 acres. They produce 225,000 bushels of white corn each year for Martha White meal, along with wheat, soybeans, milo, and tobacco.

Foreword

There was a time, not so very long ago, when *Kentucky* brought to mind not only bourbon and horses, but also tobacco. This was a time when tobacco was the state's largest cash crop, when every little farm had some tobacco on it, and before the health effects of tobacco use were fully understood. Much has changed since that time, but some things have not. As Bobbie Bryant beautifully illustrates in *Farming in the Black Patch*, the story of tobacco is not just a story about a past way of life. Tobacco remains important to many Kentucky farmers today for reasons of both economy and culture, factors not easily separated.

Dark tobacco at Smith Farms (Smith family)

Workers get their daily work assignments from farm owner, Billy Dale Smith. (Michael Breeding)

Billy Smith and his grandson, Josh, discuss the work load of the day. (Michael Breeding)

Francisco Tovar applies pollen to flowers to cross pollinate and make burley seeds. (Smith family)

This book is organized around the seasonal cycle of tobacco work. For generations, this cycle has dictated the rhythm of life on tobacco farms. Farmers may talk about planting their seedbeds around Valentine's Day, setting tobacco around or before Memorial Day, stripping tobacco on Thanksgiving, and so forth. These seasonal markers demonstrate that tobacco is as much a part of life on the farm as the holidays. At one time, the goal was to get the tobacco sold by Christmas so there *could be* a Christmas, and so that the mortgage payment could be met at the first of the year. Farmers often talk about what tobacco money has done. It paid for an engagement ring, it paid the down payment on a farm, it paid for the children's education. Farmers stress that tobacco pays for so many things that are necessary to farm families.

Workers oil tobacco at Carraway Farms. (Carraway Farms)

Workers at Smith Farms load cut tobacco onto scaffold wagons. (Bobbie Bryant)

Bernardino Ruiz displays a cured leaf of tobacco. (Smith family)

Several workers work in tandem to load cut tobacco onto the slow-moving scaffold wagon. (Bobbie Bryant)

Moving cured air-cured tobacco from the barn. (Bill Bryant)

Many types of tobacco are grown in the United States, each with a different use. Tobacco regions vary widely because of the unique growing, curing, and marketing practices involved in the production of each type and the resulting regional culture and history. The "Black Patch" is a case in point. The curing methods used by farmers today are not that different from those their ancestors brought with them when they moved to the region. As demonstrated in this fine book, dark-fired tobacco, used primarily in chewing tobacco, requires specialized knowledge at every stage. The curing, which is done by firing it multiple times, is described by farmers as an art form because a farmer must know the personality of a particular barn and judge how that personality will interact with a particular crop. As farmers are quick to say, *you can't just jump out there and do it if you've never done it*, and each year brings new challenges, as no crop is ever the same as the last.

The Black Patch also has a unique history, as it is known as the center of the Black Patch Wars of the early twentieth century. This was a period in which farmers attempted to organize in order to demand higher prices for their crop. The result was violence against farmers who were unwilling to join. Plant beds were scraped, barns were burned, and farmers were killed. The uniqueness of the region—in both the past and present—is important to the story of the Black Patch because it is key to understanding why many farmers continue to raise the crop when its social and cultural meanings have changed dramatically.

Farmers in the Black Patch often tell a story about tourists or other outsiders driving through the region who see smoke coming out of the barn and stop to warn the farmer that his barn is on fire. I have no doubt that this has happened. But we tell stories for multiple reasons, and this story also serves as an expression of how the world has changed: few understand tobacco farming today, and certainly outsiders do not.

Men load cured tobacco into hogshead to ship to market.
(William T. Turner)

Tobacco men grade tobacco at a warehouse in [illegible]
(William T. Turner)

Buyers review tobacco at the loose leaf floor in Murray, Kentucky.
(Murray State University, Pogue Special Collections)

Cut tobacco is left on the scaffold wagons, waiting to be hung in the barns. (Smith family)

The story of tobacco in Kentucky has gotten increasingly hard to tell. As the health effects have become more widely understood, the motivations of farmers have been questioned, and the state's leaders have worked to distance the image of Kentucky from tobacco in the present day. The farmers featured in this book are sixth- and seventh-generation farmers. This is part of what farmers mean when they say that raising tobacco is in their blood. It may be a surprise to some to know that there is pride in raising a good crop of tobacco, and that the nostalgia expressed in this book is felt by so many. But a good crop links these farmers to those who came before them, those who raised tobacco on the very same land, and it reminds them of who they are. It is not mindless adherence to tradition, however. These farmers have the knowledge and experience, the land, and the equipment to raise high-quality tobacco. And at least so far, they have buyers who want it. As *Farming in the Black Patch* makes clear, tobacco is heritage for many Kentuckians, but it is also remains central to the livelihood of many farm families.

— *Ann K. Ferrell*
author of Burley: Kentucky Tobacco in a New Century

Ann Ferrell, Assistant Professor of Folk Studies, Western Kentucky University (Eleanor Hasken)

Tobacco barn at Cunningham Farms (Danny Cunningham)

Flowering tobacco plant growing at the office of Smith Farms. (Smith family)

Acknowledgments

When my friend and videographer Michael Breeding first mentioned adapting the 2013 documentary *Farming in the Black Patch* to a book format, it seemed like such a simple idea. What I didn't realize at that time was that we could not generate photographs from the film. Therefore, my deepest appreciation goes to Dr. Andy Bailey, Bill Bryant, Craig and Joanna Carraway, Steve Carraway, Danny Cunningham, Anne Doran, Johnny Gingles, Shea and Scott Lowe, Mitchell Richmond, Korey Savage, Billy Smith, Billy Dale Smith, Josh Smith, William Turner, Sid Webb, Deana Wright, Marshall County Genealogical Society, Murray State University, Murray Main Street, and the Glen E. Martin Genealogical Research Center in Princeton, Kentucky, for their tremendous assistance in adding to the collection of photographs to tell this story.

To my husband, Bill, I owe the greatest amount of love and gratitude for his overall support of my writing endeavors, and his dedication in obtaining seasonal pictures of tobacco production. He is the steady force that enables me to do my projects and encourages me to keep moving forward.

With abiding love to my brother, Billy Dale Smith, I extend my heartfelt appreciation for his patience and willingness to let Bill and me hang around taking pictures while hard work was underway. A big thanks to my nephew, Josh, and to my parents, Shirley and Billy Smith, for their contribution of farm pictures. Daddy and Momma continue to be a great influence on my writing.

Film producer Michael Breeding conducts an interview for the 2013 film, *Farming in the Black Patch*. (Bobbie Bryant)

Bill Bryant taking pictures at Smith Farms (Bobbie Bryant)

Billy Smith with a crop of tobacco (Smith family)

Billy Dale Smith on the farm (Smith family)

Shirley (Chilcutt) Smith (Smith family)

Shirley and Billy Smith (Smith family)

William H. (Billy) Smith, Jr. with great-grandson, Logan Smith in 2010 (Smith family)

To the workers at Smith Farms, a huge thank-you. Their loyalty to our family is extraordinary and I'm incredibly grateful for their tireless efforts to make our tobacco crop the success it is, year after year.

A very special thanks to Dr. Susan W. Drake and three Spanish class students at Murray State University for their assistance in interviewing the migrant workers and translating the conversation into English. Meg Sumners, Josh Chambers, and Arturo Bustamante volunteered to assist with this project as an independent study. Dr. Drake developed a special curriculum so the students could work during the first part of the school year on translation exercises and practice speaking. The actual interviews occurred after the semester ended, when the workers arrived for the spring season.

On the day of the interviews, Dallas Lee Blanton, a friend of Meg Sumners, went along to videotape the interviews and MSU sent another student, Korey Savage, to take photographs on behalf of the university. Thank you, Dallas, Korey, Meg, Josh, and Arturo, for your enthusiastic interest and the professional manner in which you conducted yourselves.

Migrant workers at Smith Farms (Smith family)

Wheat field at Smith Farms (Bill Bryant)

Dr. Susan W. Drake reviews interview questions with the workers at Smith Farms. (Korey Savage)

Smith Farms worker Bernardino Ruiz and MSU student, Arturo Bustamante, talk about life on the farm. (Korey Savage)

L-R: Luis Tapia, Francisco Tovar, and Jonathan Barrera prepare for an interview with Murray State University Spanish-speaking students. (Korey Savage)

L-R: Billy Smith and William Turner during interviews for the 2013 film *Farming in the Black Patch*. (Smith family)

This book was greatly improved by the contributions of Dr. Will Snell, University of Kentucky Agriculture Economics, and Dr. Ann Ferrell, assistant professor of folk studies at Western Kentucky University. Their understanding of tobacco production and its impact on Kentucky, historically, economically, and culturally, continues to educate the public as well as inform future farmers.

Two very special friends made tremendous contributions to this book: William T. Turner, Christian County historian, and the Honorable Bill Cunningham, Kentucky Supreme Court justice. Their passion for the history of the Black Patch region continues to fuel my energy to keep these stories alive for future generations.

I wish to thank my two editors: Diana Taylor, who shares my love of the family farm, and Susan Lindsey, who shares my passion for history. Each of these ladies graciously extend their amazing talent to my writing projects, but even more importantly, they share the gift of friendship with me.

I am proud to acknowledge Acclaim Press, Inc. as my publisher. Their confidence in this project enabled me to complete this tribute to my heritage. A very special thank-you to Keith Steele and the entire staff for their kind assistance.

Photo Credits

Dr. Andy Bailey
Lynn Bartlett
Michael Breeding
Betsy Bryant
Bill Bryant
Craig and Joanna Carraway
Steve Carraway
Judge Bill Cunningham
Danny Cunningham
Anne Doran
Johnny Gingles
Scott and Shea Lowe
Marshall County Genealogical Society
Glen E. Martin Genealogical Research Center
Mitchell Richmond
Murray Main Street
Murray State University, Pogue Special Collections
Korey Savage
Smith Family
William T. Turner
University of Kentucky Libraries, Special Collections Research Center
Sid Webb
Deana Wright

Planting time at Cunningham Farms (Danny Cunningham)

Workers at Lowe Farms set tobacco. (Lowe Farms)

Workers top tobacco at Lowe Farms. (Lowe Farms)

Much-needed water is brought to the tobacco crop at Smith Farms. (Smith family)

Billy Dale Smith learns to plow the old-fashioned way, with a mule and walk-behind plow. (Smith family)

Picking up spiked tobacco at Smith Farms (Bill Bryant)

Luis Tapia places cut and spiked tobacco onto scaffold wagons at Smith Farms. (Bobbie Bryant)

Tobacco heads for the stripping barn at Smith Farms. (Bill Bryant)

Sawdust is ready for fires at Smith farms. (Smith family)

Fires are lit inside the barn at Smith Farms. (Smith family)

Bernardino Ruiz strips tobacco leaves at Smith Farms. (Smith family)

Smoking barn at Smith Farms (Bill Bryant)

Day's end at Smith Farms
(Smith family)

Introduction

Kentuckians have long been recognized for their ability to develop the highest quality products—bourbon, horses, music, and crafts. The production of tobacco, no less an art form, is a traditional signature industry for Kentucky.[1]

How Kentucky came to be known for its quality craftsmanship in tobacco production is a fascinating story. Ancient cave dwellers, European explorers, anthropologists, archeologists, historians, Indians, aristocrats, investors, slaves, and farmers all contribute to the tale. These accounts vary from ancient myths and homeopathic concoctions made by shamen to the legendary days of economic boom, the devastating times of bust, and the rich cultural landscape that marked the entire journey.

Tobacco's complicated history is as thorny as the opinions about its use today; its production has brought out the best in people, with neighbors generously help-

Smith Farms (Bill Bryant)

ing each other, and it has incited darker forces literally to the point of waging war.

Considered divine by the Aborigines, medicinal by the Native Americans, and a currency more valuable than gold to the Plymouth colonists, tobacco is a worldwide commodity developed from nature's gifts and improved by human skill.

From the early settlement of Kentucky, the state's economy was built on farming, and tobacco was the cash crop that provided a living for many of its people.

In my heritage, the phrase "Black Patch" looms large. This label was given to the region of far western Kentucky and northwestern Tennessee in the earliest settlement days. The phrase refers to the rich, dark soil of the region as well as the leaf of the dark tobacco that grows so well there. Early settlers of the Black Patch came primarily from Virginia, Maryland, and the Carolinas. Most immigrants were farmers, and they first grew tobacco for personal use.[2]

These were people of the land—farmers, planters, growers, crafters, cultivators, land holders, tenders, agriculturists, and gardeners.

My curiosity about Kentucky's farm history grew from my interest in tracking my ancestors. Trying to understand who they were and where they came from led me to a deeper understanding of how they made a living and carved out a life that led to my being in this very special place called Kentucky.

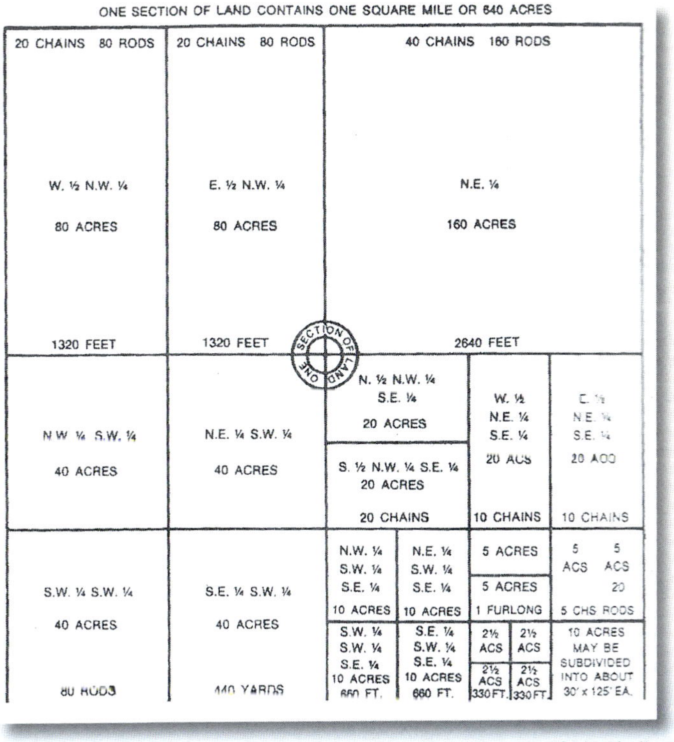

Public land survey grid of Marshall County (The History of Marshall County. Marshall County Genealogical Society)

Farm landscape in Calloway County (Bill Bryant)

"This love of the land is a common bond shared by Kentuckians," said Dr. Thomas D. Clark in *Agrarian Kentucky*. "Historically, Kentuckians have felt comfortable and cooperative with each other only in four shared ideas or experiences. The first has been common love of the land, no matter how much its appearance or productivity varied."[3]

He continued, "The land was a source of refuge and a way of life. It shaped the history of the state, flavored the culture and the politics, infused the Kentucky personality, and prospered or impoverished people with a decisive hand."[4]

Close up of tobacco (Bill Bryant)

Gravesites of Smith Farms ancestors, Henry Smith and Elizabeth (Lizzie) Staley Smith, Soldier Creek Cemetery in Marshall County (Smith family)

I learned that our first Kentucky forebear, Henry Smith, began farming here in 1832 after moving with his wife, Elizabeth, and their family from the Piedmont area of North Carolina. They had grown tobacco there, and it is likely they brought tobacco and other crop seeds with them through the Cumberland Gap into Kentucky.

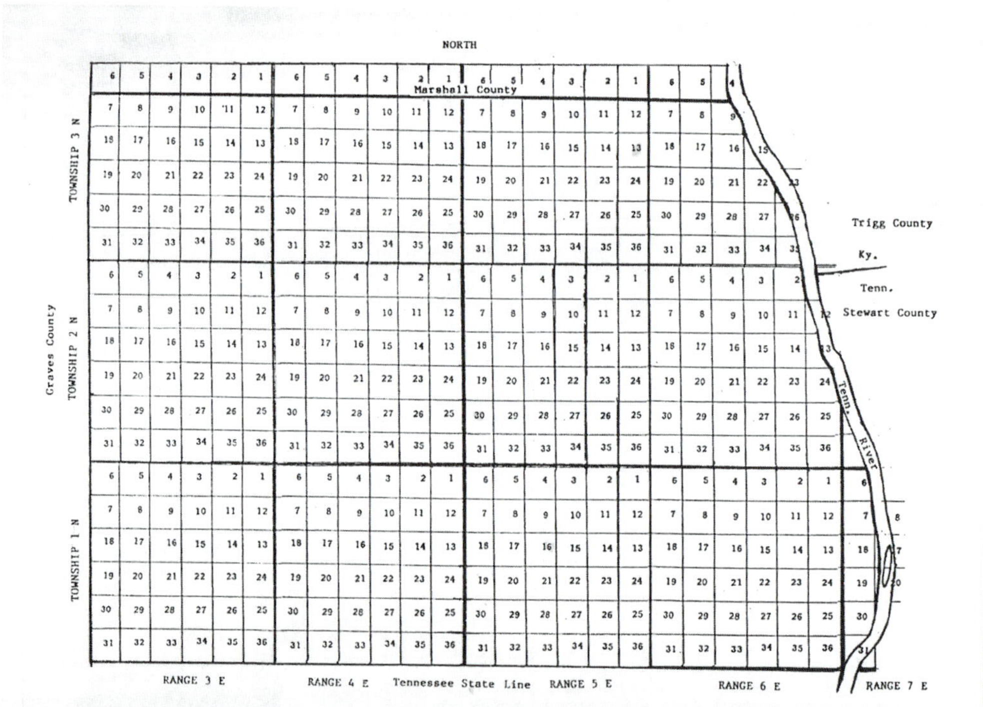

Calloway County, Kentucky plat map showing Henry Smith's property at northwest quarter section, #16 range 5, township 1, East (Map from the Kentucky Secretary of State website.)

Henry and his sons began buying property, settling close to one another in Calloway County, Kentucky. Over the years, the Smith clan settled within fifteen miles of one another, helping each other build modest homes, sheds, smokehouses, corncribs, outhouses, and milk barns. Today's Smith Farms is still within those early boundaries of property ownership.[5]

My brother, Billy Dale Smith, continues the farming tradition as a full-time farmer. Owner and manager of Smith Farms, he is the eighth-generation Smith to till this soil. In addition to growing tobacco and managing the 300-plus acres of Smith Farms, he grows corn, soybeans, and wheat on 1,200 additional acres leased in the area. He has a son, a daughter, and two grandsons following in his dusty boot steps.

Smoking tobacco barn (William T. Turner)

Farm scene in Christian County (William T. Turner)

Tobacco crop at Smith Farms (Smith family)

This book was produced to complement the production of the documentary, *Farming in the Black Patch.* The film arose from a request from Billy Dale that I help him with a special project creating something to show visitors who arrive at the farm for a tour on rainy days. My background in the communications field gave me the experience and knowledge needed for such a project.

Billy Dale knows that tobacco farming is a practiced art form, a true craft. It is a learned skill and trade—taught by one generation to the next. Sharing the complexities involved with those who are unfamiliar with tobacco production is not an easy task.

Our initial idea was to have video clips to show visitors the actual dark-fired production processes on the farm. In time, that concept turned into a much bigger idea, as we began working with film producer Michael Breeding of Lexington, a remarkable talent and storyteller.

As we talked, I learned that he also had grown up on a tobacco farm, and we agreed that tobacco farming is very different today from when we were kids. We decided this was an opportunity to convey the process of growing tobacco in a context of the social and cultural elements that made it such an important crop for so many Kentucky families.

This book shares details of the farming culture and the production of dark-fired tobacco in western Kentucky. I have relied upon local farmers and Kentucky historians to reveal the complicated production process and layers of history that make up this story.

While I no longer farm, I am still in touch with the dark soil of the Jackson Purchase[a] that nurtured my childhood and provided my family's livelihood. I am proud of my farming heritage.

It is a privilege to write about our family's farm. I can close my eyes and almost smell that dark leaf tobacco as it cures in the barn above smoldering fires. It is a comforting fragrance, a distinctive aroma that reminds me of my western Kentucky home.

—Bobbie Smith Bryant

[a]The *1998 Atlas of Kentucky* reports that the Jackson Purchase is the land located between the Tennessee and Mississippi Rivers in the far western region of Kentucky. This territory of over two thousand square miles was bought by President Andrew Jackson from the Chickasaw Indians in 1818.

Farming in the Black Patch, 2013 documentary.

Film producer Michael Breeding tapes an interview with JohnMichael Puckett at Smith Farms, September 2012. (Bobbie Bryant)

Entrance to Smith Farms
(Billy Dale Smith)

Close-up of dark-fired tobacco (Mitchell Richmond)

Scaffold wagon of tobacco ready for the curing barn (Bobbie Bryant)

Tobacco barn in Calloway County (Smith family)

Billy Dale Smith checks the barn as the fires burn below. (Michael Breeding)

Christian County farmer with cured tobacco (William T. Turner)

Garden and barn in Calloway County (Smith family)

Rich, dark soil of western Kentucky (Mitchell Richmond)

Barn with tobacco curing at Smith Farms (Bill Bryant)

Smoking barns at the Raymon Smith farm (1893-1971), the great-grandfather of today's Smith Farms owner, Billy Dale Smith. (Smith family)

A Look at the History of Tobacco

Nicotiana (By an uspecified 19th-century cigar manufacturer [public domain], via Wikimedia Commons)

There are more than sixty varieties of tobacco, but only two are important to the Kentucky story. *Nicotian*[b] *rusticum* is a small-leafed, harsh-smoking variety. The other strain, *Nicotiana tabacum*, became the basis for almost all commercially grown tobacco in the United States. This strain has larger leaves, is milder, and has a richer taste.[6]

6000 BC

Experts believe the tobacco plant, as we know it today, began growing in the Americas around 6000 BC. Its origin is the stuff of Native American myth: when the land was barren and people were starving, the Great Spirit sent forth a woman to save humanity.

As she traveled the world, everywhere her right hand touched the soil, potatoes grew. Everywhere her left hand touched the soil, corn grew. And when the world was rich and fertile, she sat down and rested. When she arose, tobacco grew where she had been seated.[7]

Indigenous people often associated tobacco with forms of religion and sometimes used it for healing purposes. The Mayas, who settled in the Mississippi Valley, smoked tobacco and spread the custom to other tribes. The Mayas believed tobacco was a sacred plant and used it as an offering to the Jaguar-Sun God in the hope that he would bring rain to their crops.[8]

[b]*Nicotiana* is the botanical name for all tobacco. The word is derived from Jean Nicot, the French scientist, physician, and ambassador to Portugal, who introduced tobacco into France in 1560.

Aztec feast. Illustration from the Florentine Codex, Late 16th century. (Wikimedia Commons)

1400

South American aborigines used tobacco as a form of hospitality and for sacred ceremonies. They believed that the aroma was a fragrance that brought favor from the Great Spirit.

Tobacco and the various ways of using it (smoking, chewing, and snuff) spread throughout the Americas, the Caribbean, and much of the globe within one hundred years of its discovery by European explorers in the late fourteenth and early fifteenth centuries.[9]

When Christopher Columbus arrived in the New World in 1492, the indigenous people offered gifts of fruit, wooden spears, and dried leaves that gave off a distinct fragrance. Those leaves were tobacco.

Columbus accepted the other gifts, but discarded the leaves. Later, however, his sailors saw the Indians "drinking" smoke and eventually had to try it for themselves.[10]

Portrait of a man reported to be Christopher Columbus, Metropolitan Museum of Art, online collection. (Wikimedia Commons)

Landing of Columbus, by American painter John Vanderlyn (Wikimedia Commons)

1500

By 1573, Sir Francis Drake had traveled to the Americas and returned to England, taking tobacco and the practice of smoking with him.[11] A few years later, he introduced tobacco to Sir Walter Raleigh, who made it fashionable.[12] Smoking a pipe became a popular pastime, albeit an unfamiliar one to some people; Raleigh was reportedly doused with water by a maid who thought he was on fire.[13]

Early users believed tobacco had medicinal qualities. It was said to cure colic, bronchial problems and toothaches, disinfect cuts, and serve as a purifying agent, sooth snake, spider, and insect bites, and was even used as toothpaste.

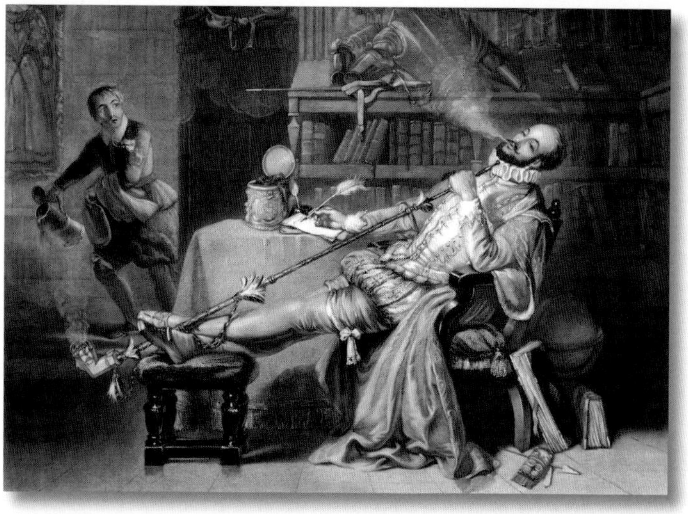

"Raleigh's First Pipe in England," an illustration included in Frederick William Fairholt's *Tobacco, Its History and Associations*. (Wikimedia Commons)

1600

The Spanish monopolized the earliest commercial cultivation of tobacco in the Americas; they exported the crop from the Caribbean to European ports. John Rolfe began growing tobacco in Jamestown around 1607 or 1608, and it soon became a mainstay of the English colony's economy.

In 1606, to keep Spain at the head of tobacco production, King Philip III decreed that tobacco could be grown only in specific locations—including Cuba, Santo Domingo, Venezuela, and Puerto Rico—and proclaimed, "The sale of tobacco to foreigners is punishable by death."[14]

By 1610, Sir Francis Bacon wrote that tobacco use in England was increasing and that it was hard to stop using it. That same year, William Barclay's *The Trial of Tobacco* was published, and provided recipes and formulations for medicinal preparations. Barclay defended tobacco as a medicine, but condemned it for casual use.

In China, meanwhile, an imperial edict forbade the planting and use of tobacco.[15]

By 1619, tobacco was used as currency or country money in the colonies—becoming literally a cash crop throughout the seventeenth and eighteenth centuries, lasting twice as long as a monetary standard as did gold.[16]

Drawing of a medicine man, Atna-Indianer, Wellcome Images, a website operated by Wellcome Trust, a global charitable foundation based in the United Kingdom. (Wikimedia Commons)

Sir Francis Drake, by Marcus Gheeraerts the Younger (Wikimedia Commons)

Francis Bacon, by unknown artist. (Wikimedia Commons)

Portrait of Philip III of Spain, Pedro Antonio Vidal. (Wikimedia Commons)

A map of Virginia and Maryland. Thomas Jefferys, Engraver R. and J. Dodsley, Publisher, New York Public Library. (Wikimedia Commons)

Loading hogsheads of tobacco at a colonial Virginia wharf. (National Park Service, Sidney King Paintings Gallery, "A Shipping Scene")

For 200 years in Virginia and 150 years in Maryland, tobacco grown by European settlers was almost entirely destined for foreign ports, where tobacco products were manufactured and sold.

1700

The first planters in Virginia became rich from growing tobacco and importing it to Europe. The laws of the land, the customs, the overall progress of the state, were all determined by tobacco.

In 1727, "tobacco notes," attesting to quality and quantity of one's tobacco kept in public warehouses, were authorized as legal tender in Virginia.[17]

When the first white settlers entered Kentucky in the late 1700s, they brought tobacco production with them, producing excessive amounts of the crop by the 1780s, when there were no nearby markets. As a result, shipping began down the Ohio and Mississippi Rivers to the Spanish port of New Orleans and from there to Europe.

The Ohio Valley became the site of a great deal of prospecting and surveying after the French and Indian War, and interest in Kentucky had grown considerably by 1774-75. As the country grew, so did production of tobacco, particularly in Maryland, Pennsylvania, North and South Carolina, and westward into Kentucky and Tennessee.[18]

Over time, new strains of tobacco were developed and eventually a darker type emerged as most suitable for the soils of central Virginia, as well as Western Kentucky and Tennessee, an area that became known as the Black Patch. The darker leaf is used to make snuff and chewing tobacco.[19]

1800

The development of steamboats and canals in the early 1800s greatly facilitated the shipping process. During the 1850s, railroads linked production and tobacco manufacturing for the first time.

The beginning of the Civil War in 1861 interrupted the tobacco trade. With the suspension of downriver trade until 1863, Kentuckians had no markets. The return to regular trade was slow; Kentucky farmers didn't have access to regular markets until 1890.

Union and Confederate soldiers sometimes socialized between battles, exchanging southern tobacco plugs for Union coffee, thus spreading "chaw" consumption northward.

Cooper's Warehouse in Christian County. Picture shows the process of sampling tobacco out of hogsheads, pronounced "hogzits." (William T. Turner)

Close up of tobacco plant (Bill Bryant)

1890–1900

In 1890, J. B. Duke, president of W. Duke and Sons, organized a consortium of East Coast manufacturers into the American Tobacco Company. American Tobacco soon became known as the Trust, and it dominated the tobacco market within twenty years.[20]

The Trust absorbed more than 250 of its competitors, often using price wars to convince manufacturers to join. Its growth coincided with lower prices for tobacco in the Black Patch area of western Kentucky and Tennessee. Soon the Trust was facing allegations of price fixing.

Tobacco farming expanded during the 1890s. Production had begun in earnest in North Carolina, but fell when cotton prices prompted many cotton growers throughout the South to turn to tobacco production.

To make matters worse for farmers, in 1898 Congress levied a new tax of $1.50 per thousand on all cigarettes and twelve cents a pound on other manufactured tobacco products, increasing consumer costs and cutting demand.[21]

James Buchanan Duke. (Wikimedia Commons)

Common Stock Certificate, American Tobacco Company. (Wikimedia Commons)

Typical tobacco barn in Calloway County
(Smith family)

Typical tobacco patch, located in Christian County (William T. Turner)

Price fixing, new competition, changes in the way tobacco was sold, and a new tax combined to spur western Kentucky farmers to action.

In the Black Patch, early efforts to organize and resist the exploitive practices of the Trust brought farmers together in protest. In time, their frustrations fueled acts of violence in what came to be known as the Black Patch War.[c]

The Black Patch War

In the 1870s, a Greenback Labor Party (a forerunner of the People's Party) emerged to provide easier access to credit. The idea was to print more money, creating an inflated currency.[22] Although the party wasn't popular in Kentucky politics statewide, it did get the attention of Black Patch tobacco farmers.

Soon after this effort failed, a new cooperative store system emerged. The Patrons of Husbandry, otherwise known as Grangers,[23] built local store cooperatives in Kentucky and Tennessee where farmers could buy necessities at lower prices. The concept was similar to modern-day big box stores where volume purchases mean lower prices. But, no matter how cheap the products were, farmers couldn't afford them.

Texas farmers, meanwhile, were trying a different approach. The Farmers' Alliance was formed in 1877 with the intent of rebuilding the American economy and relieving the agriculture debt crisis after the Civil War. This group organized sub-alliances throughout the South and West.

In essence, Alliance members created government-backed holding stations that gave low-interest loans to farmers and created cooperatives of farmers who pooled their resources and waited for higher prices. In 1886, a Texas Alliance member was sent to his hometown of Cadiz, Kentucky, to form a sub-alliance.

---

[c]See Tracy Campbell, *The Politics of Despair* by Tracy Campbell (UK Press, 1993) for a very informative and detailed account of the social, political, and cultural activities leading up to the Black Patch Wars.

In Tennessee, the first Alliance organizers appeared in 1887 and that state's first sub-alliance was formed in March 1888. By September, more than three hundred sub-alliances had been formed. From January to May 1889, the cooperative idea spread further, and Kentucky's sub-alliances doubled their membership. By the end of that year, Kentucky had more than one thousand sub-alliances.

To Black Patch farmers, the organizing core of the Alliance program was the self-help Tobacco Congress. In 1889, the Tobacco Congress met to discuss building a warehouse in Clarksville, Tennessee, to let farmers bypass the middlemen, receive fair treatment, and get better prices.

With Duke's hold on the market, farmers realized that something had to be done. In 1901, tobacco producers from sixteen Black Patch counties were called together for a meeting in Clarksville, Tennessee. They discussed several ways of coping with the tobacco industry's monopoly. Local bankers also attended the meeting. Attendees offered a mix of ideas, including a cooperative effort to increase competition among buyers. Calling themselves the Tobacco Growers Association, this group attempted to get farmers to band together to improve prices.

As prices continued to fall, tobacco farmers across the Black Patch struggled to stay afloat. Some held meetings with neighboring farmers to establish their own voluntary actions. Their moods became more desperate every day.

In 1902, John M. Foster founded the Robertson County Tobacco Growers Association in Tennessee. The organization developed a plan that later helped make the Planters Protective Association a reality throughout the Black Patch.[24]

The Tobacco Growers Association petitioned Congress to remove the tax on manufactured tobacco products. The legislative effort failed, but organizers were able to educate farmers and solicit their support for the concept of cooperative pooling of tobacco to raise prices. Local newspapers were used to spread the cooperative message.[25]

Christian County tobacco farmers with tobacco on sticks, ready to be hung in the barn for curing (William T. Turner)

"Nobody on God's earth ever raised tobacco for the sheer fun of it. In 1900, the top grade of dark-fired tobacco was bringing ten cents a pound. By 1903, it was six cents a pound. By 1906, it was three cents a pound. When it dawned on the farmers of the Black Patch that it was costing them the same amount to produce their tobacco as it was to sell it, they began to gather in droves at the railroads crossroad of Guthrie, Kentucky, where the Louisville/ Memphis division crossed the Evansville/Nashville division."[27]

—Christian County Historian William T. Turner

Christian County Historian William T. Turner (Bobbie Bryant, 2012)

Farmers then tried legal channels to indict the American Tobacco Company on antitrust charges. The Tobacco Growers Association formed a committee led by Felix Ewing to collect evidence and present its findings to the US Justice Department.

In February 1904, Ewing drafted a plan to organize farmers and invited prominent growers in Robertson County, Tennessee, to a meeting at his home. They decided to organize farmers into a crop-withholding cooperative. The plan was introduced to farmers in every county of the Black Patch, and a meeting was scheduled at the fairgrounds in Guthrie, Kentucky.[26]

William Turner recounted the event. "They went there on a Sunday, September 24, 1904, because the railroads brought the farmers of the Black Patch to a meeting attended by 5,000 tobacco farmers. Can you imagine 5,000 people in Guthrie? There they formed the Planters Protective Association (PPA), a two-state cooperative. It was in essence a U-N-I-O-N, but we farmers never used that word. And their basic idea was to create a holding action to try to drive the price up because the foundation of this whole problem was the law of supply and demand."[28]

Kentucky Supreme Court Judge and author Bill Cunningham continued the story. "It started out innocently enough with the association meeting in 1904 to form a co-op. They wanted to keep the tobacco crop off the market. They believed this action would force Mr. Duke and his tobacco Trust to pay the farmers more. It was costing about six cents a pound to grow dark-fired tobacco at that time, and they were only getting about three cents a pound. You can tell by their actions that the farmers were getting hungry."[29]

For the cooperative to be successful, an overwhelming majority of the planters needed to join the association. About 70 percent of the Black Patch farmers did join at the height of the movement. There were enough shares sold to buy warehouses, set up a marketing center, establish a headquarters, and offer cash advances for the first year's crop. Unfortunately, this was not enough to drive up prices.[30]

"Because farmers are by their very nature independent folk," Cunningham said, "some chose not to join the association at all. As it was a voluntary alliance, there were no legal means to force a farmer to join. Another disadvantage to the cooperative program was that with no more farmers joining in, there wasn't enough money to pay larger cash advances, and the pay-off from tobacco sales might take up to six months. Fortunately, the association was able to sell off the first year's crop for a good price."

Members of the association called the independent farmers Hillbillies, and there were enough of them to keep the association from being profitable. When a few leaders of the association became frustrated with the lack of full cooperation, they made up their minds to get the independent farmers to join the cooperative. This movement became known as the Possum Hunters, and it was organized as a secret society. The structure followed the lines of organizations such as the Masons and Odd Fellows, and even the Ku Klux Klan. Members were supplied with hoods, robes, and masks, and schooled in secret handshakes, ceremonies, and rituals.[31]

Dark Tobacco Growers Association, Christian County, Kentucky, ca. 1906-07 (William T. Turner)

"Most of the Night Riders were Democrats and shared the view of Confederates. Most of the Independents and Hillbillies were Republicans and Union sympathizers. We're just talking about 40 years after the Civil War. There probably weren't any veterans riding around out there, but their sons were. This was a tough bunch of guys."
—Judge Bill Cunningham

Kentucky Supreme Court Justice Bill Cunningham (Photo provided by Judge Cunningham)

Kentucky and Tennessee, like other Southern states, were going through Reconstruction. This was often a bloody and violent period. Lynch mobs were the norm in this climate of vigilantism. Given the mood of the times, night riding—moving about by horseback after dark—was not considered unusual as a way to persuade or punish people.

"Felix Ewing, along with several other farmers, decided that something must be done," said Judge Cunningham. "The association became a sort of secret fraternity and they'd have their meetings in little country schoolhouses and churches, or out in the woods. They had sentinels posted to guard against intruders or interlopers."[32]

This new insurgent group became known as the Night Riders, and was sometimes referred to as the Silent Brigade, because its members were organized in troops of armed, mounted cavalry who made their moves under cover of darkness.[33]

Somewhat surprisingly, the man who organized the original Possum Hunters into a force of vigilantes was not a farmer. He was David Amoss, a doctor from Caldwell County. He, like many other businessmen and bankers, sympathized with the farmers' plight. He saw the effort as "a fight between the working classes and the plutocracy."[34]

Amoss had attended the Christian County Military Academy and structured the Night Riders into lodges, ten to twelve men per lodge. He provided detailed instructions the night before a raid, which typically included complex rituals.

Judge Cunningham said, "They had passwords that only Night Riders knew. The sentinel would require them to say the password. A typical exchange would be a long whistle, and a long sentence, and a response. The sentinel would say, 'Have you been there?' and the key words were, 'Yes, on bended knee.'[35]

This group of marauders became legendary for their frightening appearance and vicious acts of terror inflicted upon farmers who refused to join the association. Their tactics included riding out into the night, and

Dr. and Mrs. David A. Amoss with daughter Harvey Amoss (William T. Turner)

Original Night Rider mask, on display at the Pennyroyal Area Museum in Hopkinsville, Christian County (Bobbie Bryant)

The personal residence of the Amoss family, located in Caldwell County, Kentucky (Sam Steger photograph collection, Glen E. Martin Genealogical Library, Princeton, Kentucky)

Night Rider silhouettes (Sid Webb)

burning plant beds, houses, and barns full of tobacco. They flogged some men and killed others.

Not all violence happened at night. The rift between the Hillbillies and the association members, including the Night Riders, carried over into social circles of the day. Fights would break out at church parties and school events, political gatherings, and picnics. It could happen anywhere the two opposing parties met and mingled. The situation might become even more volatile if moonshine were involved; tempers flared, and fights were almost certain to follow.[36]

For two full years, the Night Riders ran roughshod over the Black Patch region. In time, their actions became so bold that they took on entire cities. In a 2012 interview, Judge Bill Cunningham recounted the first big raid.

> In December 1906, the Night Riders made their first raid on a substantial-sized town, Princeton, Kentucky. Railroads were predominant in those days, so most of the tobacco went out by railroad or by the river. Most of the railroad towns tended to be tobacco centers, such as Hopkinsville, Princeton, Eddyville, and Russellville, in Kentucky, and Clarksville in Tennessee.
>
> So they planned a raid on Princeton where they went in nearly three hundred strong, concealed with masks, under firebrand, on horseback, and under stealth of night, they arrived around midnight. They shot up the town and took over the telephone office, taking the operator hostage.[37] They put the fire department out of service, and commandeered the local police force, holding them at bay. They burned two large tobacco warehouses, which were holding tobacco bought from independent farmers, belonging to the American Tobacco Company.

Expecting the Night Riders, Kirksey, Kentucky (Johnny Gingles)

When they left town that night, they were singing to the tune of "My Old Kentucky Home," these words: "The fires burn bright on my old Kentucky home." There was about twenty-five to thirty-five thousand dollars' worth of damage done that night, which was a huge amount for that day. That was the first raid. But the big granddaddy of them all was in Hoptown in 1907.

Hopkinsville mayor and newspaper editor, Charles Meacham (William T. Turner)

Following the same pattern they'd used successfully in Princeton, the Night Riders occupied the city of Hopkinsville with more than five hundred men in four columns of mounted cavalry. They torched a factory and a warehouse in the downtown area and destroyed more than $250,000 worth of tobacco.

Judge Cunningham recounted how Charles Meacham, mayor of Hopkinsville and editor of the local newspaper, the *Kentuckian,* was targeted during the raid.

Meacham was a scathing critic of the Night Riders. The Night Riders had a lot of popular support at that time and Meacham stood out alone in criticizing them. They were determined to go into town and play havoc with Meacham's town and destroy a tremendous amount of tobacco that was in the Trust warehouses.[38]

When the mission had been accomplished and the warehouses were all aglow, the Night Riders decided to have a little fun of their own. They began looking for Mayor Meacham to give him a good whipping. Meacham had been at home when the ruckus downtown with all the fireworks erupts. Like a good

PARTLY CLOUDY TONIGHT AND SANDAY. COLDER TONIGHT.

Daily Kentucky New Era.

Price 3c — Hopkinsville, Ky., Saturday Afternoon, December 7, 1907 — Vol. XIX. No. 12

A NIGHT OF HORROR

In Red Glare of Burning Buildings Human Devils Gloat Over Their Wanton Power In the Destruction of Property and Terrorizing of Good Citizens

Shot and Perhaps Fatally Wounded Trainman While Bravely Discharging His Duties and Brutally Assaulted Lindsay Mitchell With Butts of Guns.

THREE LARGE TOBACCO HOUSES IN RUINS

Police Station, Fire Department and Telephone Office Guarded by Members of the Mob While Their Fiendish Acts Were Being Committed

LOSS IS PROBABLY $200,000 WITH ONLY $50,000 INSURANCE

Recklessly Fired Into Private Homes and Business [illegible] and There Were a Number of Re-

Another night of crime, terror, shame and humiliation has come to Western Kentucky. A center of education has felt the hand of brutal ignorance at its throat; the land of [illegible] has permitted the terrorizing of aged and infirm [illegible] in their own homes and bed-chambers, and this in [illegible] peace. One of the most orderly cities hitherto, of its size perhaps in the south or elsewhere, has been invested by a mob from without, and the neighborly principles of the [illegible] of Christ have been violated in a home of [illegible] and literally at their doors. Strong men [illegible] another dumbly but with deep questioning in their eyes. The eyes of such seem to ask, "Is this the town of our love and pride." Tears for the severely wounded peace and honor of our section are on many cheeks, and they are amply justified by the events of last night.

Campbell and Fourteenth streets, and on way, shot at and narrowly missed Rev. George W. Means, pastor of the Methodist church, who was at the window in his residence. They fired this warehouse as they had M. H. Tandy & Company and the big building was soon a mass of flames. Tandy & Fairleigh are representatives in Clarksville-Hopkinsville tobacco district for Italian Regie.

Totally Destroyed.

Their plant and warehouse were totally destroyed, together with large quantity of tobacco. Several smaller buildings caught from flames and burned and it was with [illegible]

and citizens did magnificent work. But for these facts entire city might have been destroyed.

Beat Mr. Mitchell.

Marching down Fourteenth street to Main, about thirty men went to home of Lindsey Mitchell, buyer for Imperial tobacco company. Compelling him to come out to them, after they had riddled his room with bullets, they beat him brutally on the head with guns.

The loss occasioned by the invasion will probably reach $200,000, with $50,000 insurance.

Wrecked Front

The invaders wrecked front of Kentuckian newspaper office, of which [illegible]

ly had the invaders moved that before the fire department could get out they had surrounded the central fire station and with leveled guns kept the firemen back in the station, threatening to shoot both men and horses if an attempt was made to bring out the wagons. Ernest Hayden, one of the firemen, stuck his head out of a window and immediately one of the masked fiends shot at him but the bullet did not strike him.

Capture Operator.

From there to the L. & N. station was only a short distance, and here they captured Night Operator Will Owen and took him to the corner of Ninth and Liberty streets, where he was held under guard with several other citizens who had been captured. Prior to capturing the operator the Night Riders shot out three windows in the waiting room.

Burned Quickly.

The independent warehouse of M. H. Tandy & Co., was then fired, entrance being gained by breaking in the front door. Coal oil was used liberally and almost in an instant the entire building, which covers an entire square, was a mass of flames and from the fire here the warehouse adjoining this, occupied by R. M. Wooldridge & Co. as a storage [illegible] for the Planters Protective Association, caught and this also was completely destroyed. The warehouse occupied by M. H. Tandy & Co. belongs to John C. Latham, of New York, and the one occupied by R. M. Wooldridge & Co. was the property of W. T. Cooper.

Seeing that the Tandy warehouse was beyond saving the Night Riders marched in military array up Campbell street to the warehouse of Tandy & Fairleigh, representing the Italian Regie contractors.

Broke Into Office.

Ed. Shanklin, the watchman at this place, heard the footsteps of the men as they marched up the street and securing his gun he went down into the basement of the building. The Night Riders broke into the [illegible]

gun at the train. The entire load of shot, for it was a shotgun, took effect in Felix, back and he fell to the ground at the crossing of Ninth street. He was picked up by the train crew and on account of their being unable to secure a physician here by reason of the telephones not being available, a hurry trip was made to Crofton where Dr. S. H. Williams dressed the man's wounds. Dr. Williams found that thirty five duck shot had entered Felix body causing a most serious wound. This morning the wounded man was put on a train and carried to Nashville.

Shot at Random.

Contrary to their usual custom the Night Riders did not confine their operations to the destruction of tobacco warehouses but destroyed property in the business district indiscriminately and shot at random into dwellings in the residence section. That the masked devils cared not for life or property is shown by the many gaping bullet holes through windows and woodwork which remain as mute testimonials of their marksmanship. That many lives were not lost seems to be almost a miracle.

Not Visited.

The plants of the Imperial Tobacco company and the American Snuff [illegible]

Gray & Gaines, the Ninth street liverymen, are minus a handsome sorrel mare, a full set of harness and a black top buggy. The last seen of this rig it was being driven by two of the Night Riders.

Stole Buggy.

The buggy, in charge of Ben McReynolds, a colored boy, had been on a trip down the Clarksville pike. The boy returned to town while the Night Riders were doing their worst and he was met at the crossing of the Clarksville pike and the L. & N. railroad by a body of men. They forced the boy to stop and climbing in they drove down to the police office where they made the negro get out and they turned and drove back down Main street, this being the last

Night Rider headlines in the *Daily Kentucky New Era.*

mayor should, he went downtown and ran right into all the marauders. They recognized him, and gave chase on horseback, while he was on foot. In evading them, he ran down a dead-end alley next to the Hopkinsville Baptist Church.

When he was cornered, he finally turned to face a terrible plight. As the Night Riders were about to overtake him, out of the corner of his eye he sees a coal chute going into the basement of the Baptist Church. Now, Charles Meacham is a tall lanky guy, and he had to work at it, but he got in the chute and slid down into the basement of the church.

The Night Riders are now confronted with a dilemma. While they might not be acting like it, they were church people. These are prominent people in the community. So do they go into the church, go into holy ground and jerk Meacham out of there with violence, or do they let him go?

They decided they'd better honor God rather than their own sense of revenge, so they let him go. They had as much fun out of it as they could, because years later they said Charles Meacham was the only Methodist-sprinkled saint saved in a water-dunking Baptist Church.

The raid on Hopkinsville was carried out with great precision and great success, much like the Princeton raid, except for some notable exceptions.

The Night Riders leader, David Amoss, was wounded accidently by his own troops. They rushed him out to a little town called Wallonia

The *Kentuckian* newspaper office in Christian County (William T. Turner)

Road from Hopkinsville to Cadiz, taken by the Night Riders on their return trip home (William T. Turner)

Christian County's Tandy and Fairleigh's Tobacco Warehouse, southwest corner of 14th and Campbell Street, in ruins after the raid by the Night Riders (William T. Turner)

in Trigg County to a Dr. Hayden, a Night Rider sympathizer, who treated him for superficial wounds. But when he was carried out of Hopkinsville on a livery rig, his troops didn't know his wounds were superficial. They thought he was gravely wounded.

Amoss's last instructions to his troop were to "keep up the rear guard," which they did not. As a result, when the Night Riders made their escape down what is now State Highway 68, a couple of them were wounded and one eventually died.

In the winter of 1907, the newly elected governor of Kentucky, Augustus Willson, called out the militia (Kentucky State Guard) in western Kentucky. A month later, the Night Riders attacked the city of Russellville, destroying more warehouses full of Trust tobacco.[39] This raid drew even more militia regiments to the area.

At about the time Governor Willson was gaining control of the state, the Law and Order League began forming in Kentucky and Tennessee. These groups were well spoken, included more pleasant people among their members and were led by General Simon B. Buckner, a Confederate Civil War hero and former governor. Mayor Meacham of Hopkinsville also organized a Law and Order League, trying to calm the fears of local people. Unfortunately, this organization didn't work and in time was dissolved.[40]

Kentucky Governor Augustus Willson (Wikimedia Commons)

As the terrifying events subsided, the association's importance began to wane for two reasons. The 1907 tobacco crop generated eight cents a pound, which had been the association's target figure. In 1909, Representative A. O. Stanley got the despised tax on tobacco repealed.

Mary Lou and Robert Hollowell (Glen E. Martin Genealogical Library, Princeton, Kentucky)

A court battle waged by one of the families hurt by the Night Riders ended the Black Patch War. Mary Lou Hollowell[d] and her husband, Robert, took the Night Riders to federal court and won a judgment against them. Because of her brave act, a number of other cases were brought to trial, and many Night Riders were ruined financially or forced to leave the state.[41]

Judge Cunningham recalled the case:

> Mary Lou had a lot of fight and spunk and she ended up suing the Night Riders in federal district court. No one had ever been able to do anything in suing the Night Riders in the state court system because so many of the local population were Night Riders. A secret pass would get Night Riders on the jury so they could protect their fellow members.[42]
>
> Federal court was different, though, because in those days, it included all of west Kentucky, which they considered as Elizabethtown westward. So when Mary Lou sued in federal district court in Paducah, there were members of that jury from as far away as Elizabethtown and the Louisville area, because of it being from that district.
>
> After two tries, she and Robert got a $35,000 verdict against the Night Riders, which was huge

[d] The Hollowells' story is detailed in full in Judge Bill Cunningham's book, *On Bended Knees: The Night Rider Story.*

Kentucky State Guardsman standing guard over Milton Oliver's tobacco patch in Christian County in 1911. Mr. Oliver was a witness in the Night Rider trial. (William T. Turner)

Kentucky State Guard in Christian County (William T. Turner)

Kentucky State Guard in Murray Kentucky (Murray State University, Pogue Special Collections)

in those days. That was the beginning of the end. Because instead of the Night Riders meeting in different lodges to plan raids upon towns or beatings of independent farmers, they then started meeting to think of ways to raise the money for the thirty Night Rider defendants who had to cough up the $35,000. Ultimately, they settled for less than that.

Now the Night Riders were on the run themselves. They'd gone into this movement because of penury and definitely could not afford to have civil suits slapped on them. When Mary Lou and Robert were successful, then all the other Night Riders were sued in federal court. John Miller, the lawyer who handled their case, must have made a lot of money suing the Night Riders. Even David Amoss, the leader, was sued. They were all trying to come up with that judgment money.

In fact it was told that one Night Rider saw another Night Rider on the streets of Princeton one day, saying, "Where you been Billy Jo? I haven't seen you in a long time." He said, "I've been worming tobacco for Mary Lou"—meaning I've been trying to come up with the money to pay Mary Lou for the judgment against me.

Judge Cunningham also described the fate of Dr. Amoss.

Jury selected for the Night Rider trial in Christian County, March 1911. Seated, left to right: R. S. Lindsay, Ed B. Moss, Horace M. Henderson, F. B. Wagoner, Dan E. Foster, and E. F. Griffin. Standing, left to right: Sheriff Lowe Johnson, W. D. Hoard, J. T. West, J. R. Fears, E. H. Major, Joe Davis, John H. Williams, and Deputy Sheriff Jewell W. Smith (William T. Turner)

The revered popular leader was finally prosecuted in Hopkinsville by Commonwealth Attorney Denny Smith, who during the Night Rider heyday was considered a sympathizer with the Night Riders. But, Denny being a politician, saw the winds of politics changing. He got on the anti-Night Rider bandwagon.

The climate shifted to where those who were unpopular were no longer in danger. Some were even considered heroic. I know of no instance of where any Night Riders were harassed or run out of the state after the Night Rider movement began to wane.

Christian County Courthouse Circuit Court Room, March 1911. Trial ended the Tobacco War when the alleged leader, Dr. David Amoss of Cobb, Caldwell County, was acquitted.

When the civil judgments came down, the Lyon County Fiscal Court, the governing body of Lyon County, voted to contribute $2,000 to help pay off some of the Night Rider judgments. That's how supportive, and such an integral part they were in the community.

The Hollowells' award, along with the Supreme Court decision of 1911, breaking up the American Tobacco Company being in violation of the anti-trust laws of the US, hastened the demise of the Silent Brigade. Economic conditions improved, consumption of tobacco began to stabilize. The onerous tobacco tax was repealed, so things leveled off, economic times improved for the Night Riders, and the purpose for the association ceased to exist.

Daily Established 1888. Price 3c. Hopkinsville, Kentucky,

DR. AMOSS NOT GUILTY SAYS JURY

Verdict Was Returned Shortly After Eight O'clock Thursday Night and Only One Ballot Was Taken.

NO MORE NIGHT RIDER TRIALS THIS TERM

"We, the jury, find the defendant, Dr. David A. Amoss, not guilty as charged in the indictment."
JOHN H. WILLIAMS,
One of the Jurors.

The foregoing verdict was returned at ten minutes past eight o'clock, last night, in Christian circuit court.

It surprised nobody, for the only hope in the matter entertained by those who believed the defendant guilty was that a mistrial might result. According to one juror, only one ballot was taken.

A list of the jury follows:

John H. Williams, stock raiser; E. F. Griffin, farmer; F. B. Wagoner, farmer; M. D. Hord, farmer; E. H. Majors, farmer, Joe Davis, farmer; D. E. Foster, farmer; E. B. Moss,

DR. DAVID A. AMOSS.

the jury signified that the verdict

Daily Kentucky New Era headline announces the acquittal of Dr. David Amoss. (William T. Turner)

Sam Brewer with his grandson, Billy Smith, in Calloway County (Smith family)

Calloway County farmer Danny Cunningham in the 1980s (Cunningham family)

Typical farmstead in Christian County (William T. Turner)

Hogsheads of tobacco are moved by a forklift in Christian County tobacco warehouse (William T. Turner)

Hickory slabs used in curing tobacco (Bill Bryant)

Changes in Farming

As the twentieth century evolved, farming in Kentucky continued to evolve as well.[43]

1900	234,667 farms with 93.4 acres per farm
1920	270,626 farms with 95 acres per farm
1940	252,894 farms with 95 acres per farm
1950	218,476 farms with 89 acres per farm
1959	159,186 farms with 112 acres per farm
1969	125,000 farms with 128 acres per farm
1978	104,000 farms with 142 acres per farm
1987	99,000 farms with 145 acres per farm
1998	90,000 farms with 153 acres per farm
2000	90,000 farms with 152 acres per farm
2009	86,000 farms with 164 acres per farm

These numbers reflect the changes in farming that occurred after World War II. With mechanization improvements, fewer men returned to farming for their livelihood. In the Black Patch, once Kentucky Dam was built in 1945, new employment opportunities opened up for rural, farm families. For example, by 1988, 26 percent of Marshall County's labor force worked in some aspect of manufacturing rather than farming.[44]

Even with diminishing numbers of actual farms, there are two other factors that improved farming conditions: improved transportation systems provided easier access to larger markets and the increased use of fertilizers and chemicals increased production.

Most of the loss of farming across Kentucky occurred between 1950 and 1992.

The price of land began to increase in the early 1970s. By 1982, Kentucky farmland cost an average of more than $1,000 an acre, a price that was maintained for more than a decade.

The spillway of Kentucky Dam in the 1940s. The dam, owned and operated by the Tennessee Valley Authority, is located in northwestern Kentucky. The spillway is the largest in the TVA system, having a total discharge of over 1 million cubic feet per second. Tennessee Valley Authority. (Wikimedia Commons)

Farmland in Calloway County (Bill Bryant)

1980s to 1990s

National reports during the 1980s indicated that there was a demand for food across the globe and US farmers could fulfill it. Many farmers went broke buying too much land at inflated prices to put into food production. Although the dollar was strong, interest rates were high.

During the recession of 1982–1987, the number of Kentucky farms declined by 9 percent. The market value of equipment increased as farmers mechanized their operations.

Generally, the federal tobacco program helped stabilize the US tobacco market for many years. Farmers were provided price and income support, and there wasn't much competition from foreign markets. In the late 1980s and into the 1990s, the market changed and foreign-grown tobacco became more popular.

Additional pressures developed as tobacco quota assets were handed down from generation to generation or sold off, and more of the quota was controlled by non-growing owners. This left active tobacco growers few options other than to lease significant quantities of quota from non-growing owners.

2000

By 2001, the outlook for American tobacco production was bleak, and producers were looking for changes in the tobacco program. In 2004, federal legislation was enacted that significantly changed US tobacco policy. The Fair and Equitable Tobacco Reform Act (FETRA) became Title VII of the American Jobs Creation Act of 2004.

Commonly referred to as the Tobacco Buyout, the act repealed the federal tobacco price support and quota programs and disposed of existing pool stocks. It also paid tobacco quota owners and growers for their quota. The buyout was set over a ten-year period, with payments ending in 2014.

The act removed restrictions on who could grow tobacco and how much could be produced. There were no geographic limitations placed on production and no price support levels. These changes affected laws that had been in place since 1938.

Despite the substantial drop in tobacco production in 2005 (the first year after the buyout), the United States Department of Agriculture report of 2008 indicated that Kentucky farmers outpaced all other states in the production of burley and dark tobacco.

2010 and Beyond

Farming in the Black Patch continues to be a strong economic engine for the region, and tobacco is still a relevant crop. Given recent changes in the market with new products such as electronic cigarettes, immigration reform at the forefront of political discussion, and developing research looking at medicinal uses for tobacco plants, the future is unclear.

Dr. Will Snell, agricultural economist for the University of Kentucky, provides a look at current and future tobacco trends in the afterword of this book.

Regardless of tobacco's future, the Smith family of Calloway County will always value the controversial plant that has supported their family for more than two centuries.

Leo Carraway with grandson Craig Carraway in Calloway County (Carraway Farms)

Carraway Family Farms tobacco barn in Calloway County (Carraway Farms)

Old-fashioned well on Smith Farms
(Bill Bryant)

The People and the Plant

One hundred-eighty miles southwest of Louisville, just north of the Tennessee border, lies Calloway County and the community of Murray, Kentucky. Population: almost 18,000.

Murray is the quintessential small town with much to be proud of—a strong university with a great basketball team, an award-winning quality of life, and a thriving agricultural heritage dating to colonial times.

It is here that generations of farmers have grown dark-fired tobacco.

City of Murray welcome sign (Bill Bryant)
Above: Calloway County government seal (Calloway County Judge Executive Larry Elkins)

Cutting tobacco on the Tellus Howard farm near Lynn Grove, Kentucky. (Murray State University, Pogue Special Collections)

Farm family in Christian County (William T. Turner)

Confederate Monument at the Court Square in Murray, Kentucky (Wikepedia Commons)

Postcard of the original Calloway County Courthouse, color by Steve Caldwell (Bobbie Bryant)

Steve Carraway cuts and spikes burley tobacco at Carraway Family Farms in Calloway County. (Carraway Farms)

Typical farm landscape in the Black Patch (Bill Bryant)

Farmers cut and spike tobacco in Calloway County in the 1950s. (Smith family)

Nicotiana tabacum blanco, plate from a book. Francisco Manuel Blanco (O.S.A.) (Wikimedia Commons)

Murray is located in the heart of a region commonly referred to as the Black Patch; the name refers to both the dark soil and the dark tobacco that grows in it.

The Mississippi River flows to the west, the Ohio River to the north, and Tennessee River to the south of the Black Patch—one of few places in the world where the dark leaf variety of tobacco has been grown and where production continues today.

Early pioneers discovered that the area now known as Calloway County was blessed with particularly fertile soil.

Shirley (Chilcutt) Smith learned about tobacco after marrying a farmer. (Smith family)

Craig Carraway stands in a field of burley tobacco. (Carraway Farms)

Tobacco seeds (Mitchell Richmond)

"The people who moved into western Kentucky came from the tobacco-producing states—from Maryland to Georgia," said Christian County Historian William T. Turner. "They brought with them the knowledge, the know-how, and the techniques of raising tobacco. When folks initially settled in the area and sent word back east that the land was very rich and productive for raising tobacco, it motivated others to want to migrate westward."[45]

Immigrants brought tobacco seeds from their farms in the east. An unusual and potent variety of the crop evolved due to the minerals, soil, and climate of this western land. The new strain was called dark tobacco.[46]

A farmer's view from the tractor (Mitchell Richmond)

The variety is very different from burley, perhaps the most commonly known type of tobacco, which is used in cigarettes and marketed worldwide. This darker, heavier leaf tobacco is used for chewing tobacco and snuff. One of the most obvious differences from burley is found in the curing process for dark tobacco, which takes place inside closed barns with smoldering fires of sawdust and oak or hickory slabs.

For many generations, farmers grew only enough tobacco for personal use, but its value was apparent even in the earliest days of production. Before the Revolutionary War, debts were paid to the king with tobacco. In time, for places like Calloway County, tobacco became the most important economic engine for local residents. It was the primary cash crop.

After the Revolutionary War, migration increased westward into Kentucky. Most families settled along riverbanks, often clustering around small villages or towns.[47] From those pioneer days until the mid-nineteenth century, nearly everyone in western Kentucky farmed for a living.

Smoking barn in Christian County (William T. Turner)

Smoking barns at Smith Farms in Calloway County (Smith family)

Smoking barn in Christian County (William T. Turner)

Fires inside barns, curing tobacco (Mitchell Richmond)

Preparing barns with wood slabs and sawdust to begin the curing process at Carraway Family Farms (Carraway Farms)

Continuing the Tradition

Dark-fired tobacco is grown in only a handful of places in the world—in pockets of Europe and Africa as well as western Kentucky, central Tennessee, and southwest Virginia. It is a crop that means the world to farmers in Murray, Kentucky. Billy Dale Smith is one of these farmers.

Billy Dale is the steward of the land that his family has farmed for eight generations. He learned from his grandfather and father how to produce dark tobacco. He continues to teach his son the nuances of tobacco production and hopes his grandsons will enjoy farming when they grow up.

Although family farms are disappearing in some areas of the country, agriculture still reigns supreme in the Black Patch, and conversation never strays far from farming concerns—a learned craft and skill passed along from one generation to the next. The crop is ill-suited for someone who has never been in a tobacco field.

Billy Dale Smith with daughter Janae at Smith Farms (Smith family)

Four generations of farmers at Smith Farms. L-R: Billy Smith, Josh Smith, Billy Dale Smith and children, Logan and Carter Smith (Smith family)

Left: The iron dinner bell (Bill Bryant)

A wagon load of tobacco sticks are ready to go to the field where cut tobacco will be placed on them, and taken to the barn for curing. (Bill Bryant)

Traditional tobacco barn at Smith Farms (Bill Bryant)

Plowed field in the Black Patch of western Kentucky (Bill Bryant)

Farm children take part in the day-to-day activities of the tobacco growing season. Here, Cesar Contreras, Sayler Lowe, and Salvador Cervantes take a moment for fun during a busy day at Lowe Farms. (Lowe Farms)

Billy Dale Smith with his dad, Billy Smith (Smith family)

Noby Carraway helps his son Steve load scaffold wagons at Carraway Family Farms. (Carraway Farms)

Jonathan Barrera shows Logan Smith the right way to set tobacco plants. (Josh Smith)

Billy Dale Smith with his dad, Billy Smith (Smith family)

"It's more of an art form, I think," Billy Dale said. "You need years of experience, either from trial and error, or from it being passed down from other generations to you. It seems that I still learn something new every year. There are lots of long, grueling hours in the field and in the barns. You have to work both day and night to make a crop. I've heard old-timers say that growing tobacco is a thirteen-month-a-year job because in the past, you would be starting a new crop before you were finished with last year's crop."[48]

H. Glen Doran, a retired farmer and local banker, noted the importance of having a special talent. "There is a lot of skill to firing tobacco, particularly the skill of how you get the tobacco color set," he said. "Years ago, there was a lot of pride with farmers as to who the best tobacco grower was and who could get the best color, get the best dollar. They'd sit down at the country store and talk about their neighbor and brag about who got the best dollar for their crop. It all went back to the skill; there's a real skill in raising dark-fired tobacco. The only way to learn it is to do it, or have someone teach you. You can't learn it out of a book."

Seventh-generation farmer Steve Carraway echoed that view. "My dad grew it, and my grandfather. I've learned a lot from them. Now, my son, he's learning from me. Dark-fired is one of those crops—you can't jump out there and do it if you haven't ever done it before."

"It was our livelihood when I was growing up," added Danny Cunningham, a neighbor. "My dad had a small farm, and he grew three or four acres of tobacco, charged everything at the grocery store and at the fertilizer plant to make the crop, and then at the end of the year, we would go and pay it off."

Air-cured tobacco hangs in the barn at Cunningham Farms in Calloway County. (Danny Cunningham)

Billy Dale, Glen, Steve, and Danny have many common bonds, and one readily senses that farming is in their blood.

It is unusual these days, but some people still take up farming for the first time. They, in particular, must learn the details of the craft from someone else. Growing up in the Black Patch, Scott Lowe occasionally helped other farmers in the fields but never farmed on his own. In time, he decided to try it for himself.

"I've been fortunate enough to have a good neighbor to teach me," he said. "His name was Charles Burkeen. He's passed away now, but he showed me the ins and outs of a good tobacco crop. He'd be in the barn with me, and he'd hold his hands up and make me feel the

Danny Cunningham and his soybean crop at Cunningham Farms (Danny Cunningham)

Danny Cunningham with Lane, his great-grandson (Danny Cunningham)

Steve Carraway at Carraway Family Farms in Calloway County (Carraway Farms)

Scott Lowe cuts and spikes tobacco at Lowe Farms. (Lowe Farms)

Calloway County farmer Scott Lowe during the 2013 filming of *Farming in the Black Patch* (Bobbie Bryant)

tobacco. He showed me how to fire tobacco and how to feel it to know when it was ready."

"I actually purchased our first acres of ground from him. After he was gone, I'll admit, I've had some mess-ups. I've greened barns, you know, maybe not waited long enough for the tobacco to yellow. But, you live and learn, and you become a better farmer by learning from your mistakes."[49]

Scott recounted his first year of tobacco farming with pride. "With my first tobacco crop, I was able to purchase a wedding ring and some land to put a double-wide trailer on—that was two acres worth of tobacco. Well, it was actually just enough to buy a wedding ring and make a down payment."

There were some who thought the tobacco buyout would bring an end to production, as burley and dark-fired tobacco growers abandoned the practice. But it has been many years now since the buyout took effect, and both crops remain viable in Kentucky. For many of these farmers, it was difficult to let go when the crop had been in their blood and on their land for generations.

The farmers in Calloway County are not much different from their ancestors. They are making a living off the land. Some may wonder why, because raising tobacco, especially dark-fired tobacco, is a difficult and dirty job. Producing a tobacco crop requires more hand labor than any other major agricultural endeavor. Farm crews may have to put in more than 300 hours of labor per acre to grow a crop.

Compounding the problem is that it has been difficult to get enough help in recent years. The hard labor doesn't appeal to local workers. To make ends meet, some farmers must work a day job and then work the land on nights and weekends.

"I wouldn't do anything else but farm," Danny Cunningham said, "but it's not easy. A lot of people think it is."

Barn at Smith Farms in Calloway County (Bill Bryant)

The Smith family continues a long line of farming in the Black Patch of Calloway County.

Billy Smith with his red belly Ford tractor in the 1950s (Smith family)

Hal Smith, father of Billy Smith, with a 5000 Ford tractor, farming at Kirksey in the 1970s (Smith family)

Billy Dale Smith at Smith Farms (Smith family)

Josh Smith with son, Logan, at Smith Farms (Bobbie Bryant)

Old log barn in Calloway County (Deana Wright)

Planning for the Season Ahead: Finding Help

It's February and Billy Dale's thoughts have turned to the new growing season that lies ahead.

His greatest concern is finding workers to help with his tobacco crop. "In the early years, farmers counted on their family members to help with the farm, particularly working tobacco. I don't remember exactly what year it was, but I'd say it was in the early '90s, it started getting harder to get local help for seasonal work. Tobacco work has always been hard work. It still is. I finally started getting migrant workers to come in here. I used a broker out of Texas the first couple of years, then I started using the H-2A program."

H-2A is the type of visa required to enter the United States for seasonal work. To bring in foreign workers, a farmer must be certified through the US Department of Labor, and meet several other requirements, such as providing housing and transportation while the worker is employed on the farm.[50]

Workers at Smith Farms topping tobacco (Smith family)

Billy Dale Smith at work in his office at Smith Farms (Bill Bryant)

L-R: Clay, James, and Sam Brewer. Sam was Billy Smith's grandfather, James was his great-grandfather, and Clay, his uncle. (Smith family)

Workers at Smith Farms cutting tobacco (Smith family)

L-R: Tyler Boggess and Kyle Tracy pull pollen from male burley plants to be used in cross pollinating burley tobacco at Smith Farms. (Smith family)

A worker moves slabs at Smith Farms. (Bill Bryant)

Orlando Guzman Estrada lifts tobacco to the top tier at Carraway Family Farms. (Carraway Farms)

Workers enjoy spending time with the Smith family. L-R: Bernardino Ruiz, Billy Smith, Shirley Smith, Luis Tapia, Miguel Pineda, and Raul Hernandez.

The tobacco crop grows at Carraway Family Farms. Carraway Farms

"Most of my H-2A workers have been helping me for a really long time," Billy Dale says. "I've got four who have been helping me for ten years or longer. Last year, I had two new ones. And then, I've got a couple of boys[e] who have been helping me for three or four years. I've been real tickled with the work they have been doing and I think they have been real tickled to have a job here."[51]

For this crop year, Billy Dale selects eight Mexican workers from the migrant program; seven are confirmed and five of them have worked for the Smith family before. For them, the Smith Farm is like a friendly and comfortable home away from home. Work on the Smith Farm each year means a generous paycheck—much more than they can earn back home.

[e]The word "boys" is commonly used as a regional, colloquial term to describe farm workers of any age or race. It is considered affectionate and familial, and is in no way intended as disrespectful.

Bunkhouse for migrant workers at Smith Farms (Bill Bryant)

Visitors to the Lowe Farms get a close up view of the crop. (Lowe Farms)

Billy describes the relationship with the migrant workers. "I guess to us we consider this still a family farm. These migrant workers just become part of the family. They will eat with us occasionally, or they'll grill something for us. Or, sometimes we'll all go out to a restaurant and we'll eat together."

Farmer Steve Carraway agrees. "We've had workers for the past eight to twelve years now, and they become almost like family to us. We know their kids and their names, their wives. We keep up with their family activities in Mexico. We consider them family, really and truly."

Shea Lowe explains their family's relationship with the migrant workers. "Starting about February, our two girls ask daily, 'When are the boys coming home?' Yes, *home* is exactly what they mean. My girls assume this is their home. Since [the girls were born], the guys have been living and working on our farm. My girls only know them as part of their family. And when the boys do come home to Lowe Farms, the first tradition is our yearly family portrait. Smiles and hugs get passed around as the girls now are at ease that their family is back at one place for another year of work and harvest."[52]

The workers also speak of personal relationships. Francisco Tovar Gonzáles says, "With the time I have had here at Smith Farms, every year I come here, I almost consider myself like a member of the family precisely because the boss is a good person."[53]

Luis Tapia, Francisco Tovar, Billy Smith, Jonathan Barrera, Bernardino Ruiz and Billy Dale Smith enjoy supper together. (Smith family)

Cesar Conteras gets a snack from Sayler and Sayde Lowe at Lowe Farms. (Lowe Farms)

The Lowe family welcomes the workers back to Kentucky, just in time for tobacco season. L-R: Oscar Lomeli, Jose Felix, Scott Lowe (back center), Leonel Madera, Cesar Contreras, Salvador Cervantes, and Jose Luis Hernandez Garcia, in front, Joanna, Sayler and Sayde Lowe. (Lowe Farms)

Workers at Smith Farms load cut tobacco onto scaffold wagons. (Smith family)

Francisco Tovar interview with Spanish-speaking students from Murray State University. (Korey Savage)

Jonathan Barrera interview with Murray State University Spanish-speaking students. (Korey Savage)

Luis Tapia interview with Spanish-speaking students from Murray State University. (Korey Savage)

Bernardino Ruiz interview with Murray State Spanish-speaking students. (Korey Savage)

José Jonathan Barrera Jiménez concurs. "I feel like part of the family now, because I've been here seven years. I've done a few small things that didn't turn out right at work, and they tell me things like what I have to do, what I don't have to do, but not in a chastising way, just a point of view to do things better. There are a few things, like in a family; they don't scold you like an employee."[54]

The workers also discuss their need for the work. "I've been working for Bill Smith for sixteen years," said José Luis Tapia Rodriguez. "I like everything about Bill. He gives me a job, and my job is secure with him. I have achieved a lot of things thanks to the job I got from him and to the effort I put on it. And more than anything, keeping my job is what helps my family all the time."[55]

Bernardino Ruiz Cardenas of Guanajuato, Mexico, adds, "When I came back to the States, my family wasn't happy, because they didn't want to be alone. I spend very little time with them, and they want me to stay longer. But the necessity of progress, of doing more on my house—that is why I came to America. To provide everything they need and never have them miss food at the table."[56]

Jonathan says, "When I was a boy in Nayarit, Mexico, my house was next to a farm and they grew tobacco there. That's where I learned about tobacco. I watched, but didn't work with it. I only watched how it was worked, how to do the work. I didn't know how to work in it, but I had a pretty good idea. Here [at Smith Farms] is where I learned how to work with tobacco."[57]

Bernardino has been coming to Smith Farms for seventeen years and enjoys the work of tobacco. He also brings some knowledge from his own farm in Mexico. "Yes, I have similar work there, corn and beans." He adds that before coming to Kentucky, he had not worked in tobacco.[58]

The workers do find time to relax, however. Luis says, "Well, there's not much free time, in fact, just in the afternoons, we have time. We make food and everything, bathe, and get ready for bed. On the weekend, on Sundays, we go grocery shopping. Sunday is when we rest and go shopping."[59]

Francisco adds, "The free time would be from 6 to 8 p.m. We talk to our wives over there [in Mexico] and there's a half hour or an hour, but we do not talk to them every day, but just one, two, or three times a week."[60]

Workers at Smith Farms take a well-deserved break after a long, hot day in the field. (Bill Bryant)

Jonathan Barrera and Donaciano Arce play cards to relax after a long day in the field. (Smith family)

Raul Hernandez and Jonathan Barrera prepare dinner at Smith Farms. (Smith family)

Workers at Lowe Farms load tobacco onto scaffold wagon. (Lowe Farms)

Bernardino Ruiz and Francisco Tovar apply pollen to flowers, cross pollinating to make burley seed at Smith Farms. (Smith family)

Billy Dale Smith and Rob Ed Parrish work on equipment at Smith Farms. (Smith family)

Farm work continues for farmer Scott Lowe with equipment repairs. (Lowe Farms)

Managing a commercial farm is an all-encompassing job, and financial success can be elusive; it is certainly not recommended for the inexperienced.

"You ask different people what they've got in a crop, you'll get different answers from each one of them," Billy Dale says. "Right now, I am projecting it costing me about $7,500 an acre to put out each acre of tobacco for this year [2012]. That can change daily depending on any type of problem we have, but on the planning of putting this crop out, it figured out right at $7,500 an acre. I'm going to have to average 3,000 pounds per acre to pretty well break even."

Billy Smith with his son, Billy Dale in corn field (Smith family)

Billy Dale and his son, Josh, discuss the years tobacco crop. (Michael Breeding)

Truck driver David Emerson and one of Smith Farms tractor trailers (Bill Bryant)

Danny Cunningham with two workers at Cunningham Farms (Danny Cunningham)

Billy Dale has had the benefit of great-grandparents and grandparents to instill in him the commitment and dedication to farm life. He continues to defer to his dad for advice and is working to pass along his own experiences to his son, Josh.

William H. (Billy) Smith, Jr. is Billy Dale's father. He is proud of his son's management and accomplishments on the farm. "It's a big operation. Billy Dale is the owner and manager of the farm. He has an assistant manager who works with him year-round. He has a tractor-trailer truck driver who works whenever there is something to do. Then he has another gentlemen who runs the combines and spray rigs when we need him. Then, on top of that, he employs about eight or nine migrant workers out of Mexico."

Money isn't the only thing at stake for these farmers. A farmer's reputation can make or break a tobacco company contract and the number of acres of tobacco the buyers want can change from year to year. They know who the good farmers are, so if farmers have excellent credentials and perhaps a little luck, their acreage could be increased. If not, their contract quota could be cut.

This year, Billy Dale is growing twenty-eight acres of dark-fired tobacco. But he'll also plant 1,200 acres of soybeans, 500 acres of corn, and 110 acres of wheat. These numbers vary from year to year and are subject to market demands. If the weather cooperates, the Smith Farm will have a good year.

Spray rig at Smith Farms (Bill Bryant)

Tobacco barn at Smith Farms (Bill Bryant)

The Season Begins: The Plants

Every good crop of tobacco begins with quality plants. Local greenhouses now produce disease-resistant plants in a controlled environment, but in the past, when families grew only a few acres of tobacco, everyone raised their own plants from seed.

The elder Billy Smith shared his personal experience. "Years ago, a large tobacco crop was about five acres for a farm. Around mid-February, the farmer cut brush, piled it up, and burned a place for a plant bed.[61]

Freshly planted tobacco slip (Lowe Farms)

Tobacco plants reach for the sun from the dark soil of western Kentucky. (Lowe Farms)

"My granddad, Sam Brewer, would select three or four of the biggest and healthiest looking plants in the field of tobacco and would not top [remove] the flowers. When tobacco cutting time came he left those few plants in the field. After the harvest, he cut the seed heads, which by that time had matured. He took them to the house, or some other safe place, for the seed to continue to dry out.

"At a later date, after drying completely, he pulled the seed pods off the plant and shook the seeds out into a dish. After more days of drying he saved the seed until about mid-February."[62]

Tobacco seeds are miniscule—more than 300,000 seeds to an ounce.[63] Their small size requires them to be sown ahead of planting time to grow small plants that will transfer easily to the field. Before the 1980s, farmers created plant beds for this purpose.

Tobacco seeds ready for planting (Mitchell Richmond)

Samuel Tilford Brewer (1890-1970), great grandfather of Billy Dale Smith. (Smith family)

Typical tobacco bed in Christian County (William T. Turner)

Until mechanization, farmers prepared land for planting with a horse or mule and a walk-behind plow. (Murray State University, Pogue Special Collections)

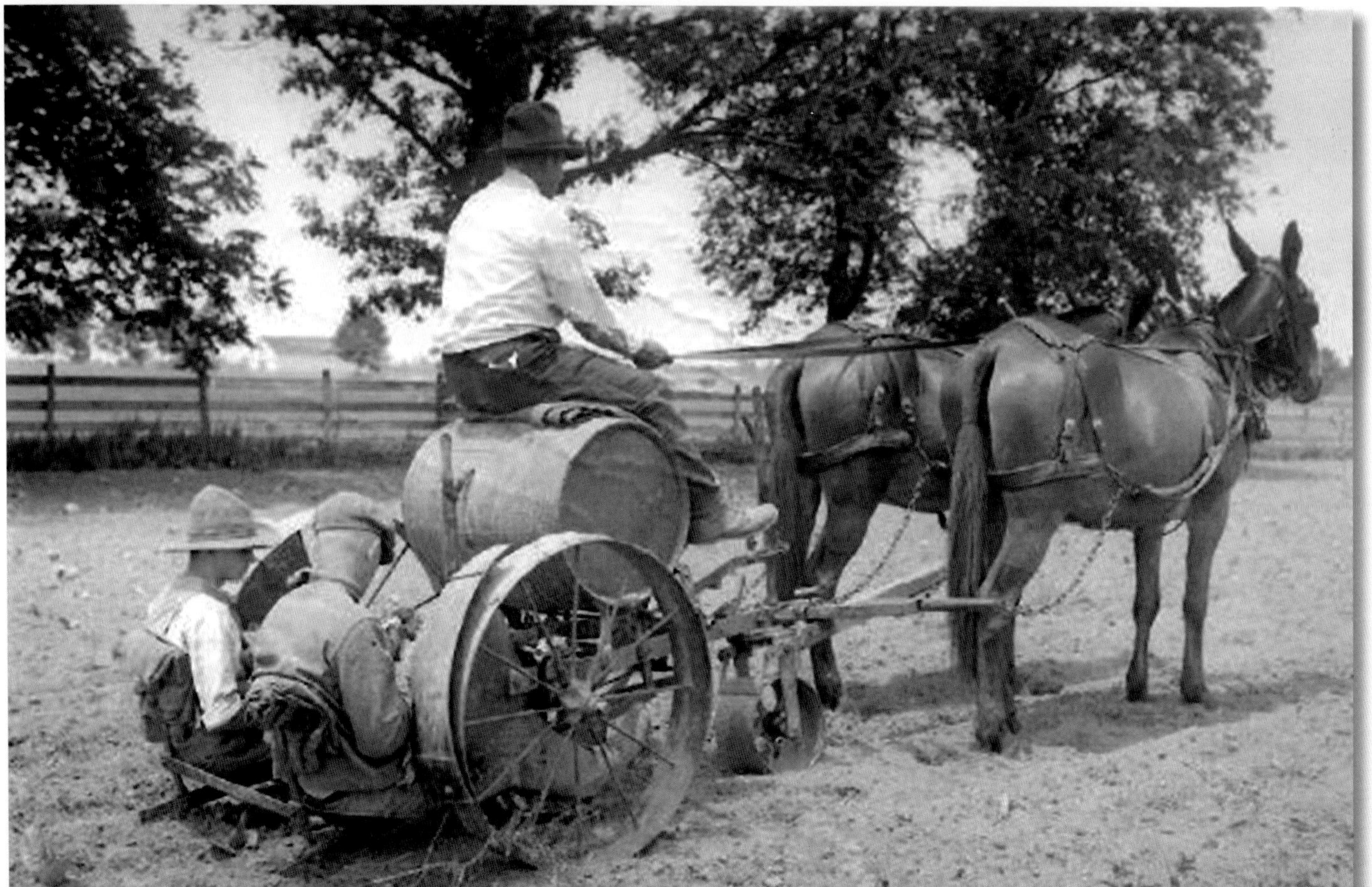

As America became more industrialized, machines were developed to aid the laborious process of hand setting tobacco. Here a mule-drawn setter is used with two workers setting tobacco slips. (University of Kentucky Libraries, Special Collections Research Center)

Tobacco seeds are often coated to make them easier to handle. Three colors are shown here in comparison to the miniscule uncoated brown seeds of tobacco. (Mitchell Richmond)

Today, farmers use motorized equipment to prepare the land for setting tobacco. (Smith family)

L-R: Luis Tapia, Bernardino Ruiz, Jesse McCallon, and Josh Smith hoe long rows of tobacco at Smith Farms, breaking up the dirt and chopping out weeds. (Smith family)

Steve Carraway remembers the process of sowing a plant bed. "When I was a kid, you used to go out to the edge of the woods and pick a warm spot. Maybe on the south side of a rolling hill, or where the water would get off of it, but it would get warm real quick. You'd try to sow a plant bed somewhere around Valentine's Day."[64]

Plant beds were generally six to twelve feet wide by thirty to 150 feet long, depending on how many acres of tobacco were to be set.[65]

"The plant bed soil was burned off to kill the existing weeds and grass seed," Billy Smith adds. "Papa Brewer would work the plant bed soil shallow and fine. He'd then take a tablespoon of tobacco seed and mix it with a small bucket of ashes and sow the seed by hand. He'd try to get over the plant bed twice so there would not be any skipped spots.

"He would then cut long logs, six to ten inches in diameter, and position them around the plant bed to hold the canvas off the ground. Once planted, the entire bed was covered with canvas. The seeds were left to grow for the next three months and the canvas would stay on the beds until the risk of frost was past.

"When conditions were right, usually by mid-May, they would go to the beds in the mornings and draw or pull plants by hand. You were usually on your knees or stooped over, which was a back-breaker, pulling one plant at a time until you had enough to set that afternoon. The number of plants to be pulled depended upon on how many people they had to help set."

The tobacco plants, or slips, were pulled by everyone, including children. They were then placed in big washtubs in preparation for setting.

Tobacco slips grow from seeds in specialized greenhouses. (Mitchell Richmond)

Logan Smith waters young slips of tobacco in preparation of setting. (Smith family)

Greenhouses full of tobacco slips ready for planting (Mitchell Redmond)

Prior to machine setters, farmers set each plant of tobacco using a wooden peg. The process was called pegging tobacco.

Bernardino Ruiz plows the field next to the newly planted corn plants, aerating the soil, so water can penetrate to the roots. (Smith family)

Craig Carraway says, "As a small boy, I can remember helping with that process, and it was tough. You would spend three-fourths of a day pulling enough plants to set just a little bit of tobacco. You were basically worn out before you ever got to the field."[66]

In the early days, farmers began clearing the land by guiding a plow behind a mule or horse. Each row was then defined with a hoe.[67]

"Usually they wanted to have the soil prepared for setting with the rows crossed with a two-row corn planter, or other marker, so you could set the plants in a 38- or 40-inch square," Billy Smith says. "Usually you would set the plants after a good rain or just in front of a good rain, so you had a better chance of getting a good stand and not having so much resetting to do."[68]

Workers brought plants from the beds and, using a hand-hewn wooden peg, stooped or bent over to place the plant, or crawled along the rows putting each plant in place, about forty inches apart.[69] Billy explains the process. "You would take a tobacco peg and make a hole in the dirt, then set the single plant in it. Then you'd gently push the dirt around the little plant and try not to injure it as you would have to come back the next week and reset it if it died.[70]

"By setting the plants in a square with 38- or 40-inch rows, they could take a mule and a harrow, or some other implement, and work the ground in both directions, eliminating a lot of hoeing and other hand labor. There were no herbicides in those days, so weeding was important. Today, these procedures have completely changed as plant beds and tobacco plants are 99 percent commercially grown and purchased by the local farms."

Oscar Lomeli and Leonel Madera set tobacco at Lowe Farms. (Lowe Farms)

Riding the tobacco setter at Lowe Farms (Lowe Farms)

Sayde (age 9) and Sayler (age 7) Lowe, at Lowe Farms, trying out the setter. (Lowe Farms)

Summer at Smith Farms (Smith family)

Chopping weeds at Smith Farms (Smith family)

Above: Beautiful field of tobacco (Smith family)

Right: The view from the driver's seat (Mitchell Richmond)

The Planting Schedule: Weather Permitting

After Billy Dale has ordered the 115,000 tobacco plants needed to set twenty-three acres of tobacco, he can begin thinking about getting the first crop in the ground by the middle of May. The timing is critical since he plans to double-crop this year, letting him grow more tobacco without needing to build more barns.

"I like to start setting tobacco the second or third week in May," he says. "We want to set four to eight acres per week, depending on the size of the overall crop, and if we are going to have to double-fill any barns. We space the setting out like this so it isn't all ready to top, oil, sucker, or cut at the same time. Also, if we are double-filling any barns, we have to set one crop early in May and the next crop in the last half of June. In doing this, we will be making better use of the workforce.

"The first crop should be ready to top and oil anywhere from around July fourth to the middle of July and ready to cut in about six to eight weeks after topping, depending on the weather we have. The second crop would normally be ready to top and oil in the latter part of August or first part of September and ready to cut in the first couple of weeks of October.

Freshly turned dirt ready for setting tobacco (Smith family)

A worker at Smith Farms disks several acres in preparation for setting tobacco. (Smith family)

Disking in early May (Smith family)

"With double cropping, you could find us cutting one field today, and topping and oiling another field the next day or even the same day. The end of August through the middle of October is a very hectic time, making sure everything works out. We want to get both crops through the barns before a killing frost."[71]

The weather is the greatest concern for every farmer. Some use the *Farmer's Almanac* for guidance, but most now use the Internet. The sophisticated tracking capabilities available today help farmers stay one step ahead of quickly changing weather patterns, but even cutting-edge technology can't always effectively predict what nature might do—and when.

This particular year (2009) starts off badly. An ice storm devastates the state, leaving piles of debris that have to be cleared before the fields can be prepared for planting.

Weather radar shows the onslaught of the 2009 ice storm.

Images of ice storm aftermath (Smith family)

Images of ice storm aftermath (Smith family)

Images of ice storm aftermath (Smith family)

Since wood chips are needed to build curing fires for the barns, Billy Dale purchases a chipper and turns the downed limbs into a useable commodity.

"The ice storm that came in the last week of January of this year, they say was the largest natural disaster that western Kentucky has had since 1811–1812 when they had the [New Madrid] earthquakes. That was when the Mississippi River ran backwards," Billy Smith says. "We had freezing rain on Sunday night, all day Monday, and Monday night. Most of the power went out in this part of the country late on Monday afternoon and during the night. We got up Tuesday morning and it was a disaster. There was ice everywhere you looked."

Craig Carraway recalls, "My son was three or four years old. I assumed the power was going to go out at the farm, so we fled to Murray to a hotel that night thinking Murray would be fine. We woke up the next morning and there was no power in Murray, and it had gotten really bad. I told my wife to pack and we headed further south. There was limbs breaking in the yard and we gathered up a bag and went to Clarksville [Tennessee] to stay at another hotel. I remember the entire parking lot was full of license plates from Kentucky."

"We actually had a generator," says Steve Carraway, Craig's dad. "We stuck it out on the farm [so we could] kind of keep an eye out on the equipment. It was tough."

"We have an 18,000-kilowatt generator on the farm," Billy Smith says. "Billy Dale got it out that afternoon and got it running. We soon had power at the house and water. Billy Dale had decided that there was so many people that did not have power and they did not know when they would get their water and lights back on, so he went down to the country store and put out word that we had two showers, two washing machines and dryers in the bunkhouse if anybody wanted to come take showers, wash clothes, do whatever they wanted to do. They were welcome to use the bunkhouse. Well then, immediately a line formed. For two days we had people washing and cooking and taking showers in the bunkhouse."

Before a crop can be planted, the fields must be cleared of all debris. After the ice storm, most of the fields are almost impassable. Billy Dale runs three crews to saw, stack, chip, and remove the wood.

"It was a very expensive storm," says Scott Lowe.

Bad weather continues to hamper progress. A wet early spring keeps farmers out of the fields, jeopardizing not only the tobacco schedule but other crops as well. At last the rains stops and farmers in far west Kentucky are able to begin setting tobacco.

A burley tobacco drying shed awaits the next crop (Smith family)

The tobacco setter Billy Dale uses is large and seats eight people, meaning four rows of tobacco can be set at a time, or eight rows on one round-trip across the field. Workers on the setter sit with their backs to the tractor that pulls it, feeding plants into a continually rotating wheel. The wheel has a mechanized clamp that grasps each plant one at a time. As each plant is set into the ground, the setter provides a shot of water and fertilizer.

Right: Preparing to set tobacco with an eight-row setter (Smith family)

Setting tobacco at Smith Farms (Smith family)

Setting tobacco takes practice. There is a rhythm to the pace of the setter, and even the youngest in the family is taught how to ride the setter early in life.[72]

It's the third week of May and the goal is to set four to eight acres of tobacco a week. Billy Smith and grandson Josh pitch in along with other part-time workers at Smith Farms. Josh, a teacher and football coach by day, helps his dad, Billy Dale, on the farm in the afternoons and on weekends.

Left: L-R: Kyle Tracy, Tyler Boggess, Luis Tapia, Bernardino Ruiz, Elliott Lovett, Nick Calhoun, Jordan Bumpus, and Josh Smith load the tobacco setter with slips for setting. (Smith family)

Bernardino Ruiz plows recently set tobacco plants at Smith Farms. (Smith family)

Tractor at Smith Farms (Bill Bryant)

A fertilizer spreader at Smith Farms (Smith family)

Equipment used for drilling soybeans or wheat (Smith family)

Combined wheat is dumped into a truck at Smith Farms (Smith family)

The workers set thirty rows of tobacco in a little more than two hours, stopping only when the plants run out. In all, they plant seven acres of tobacco this day—one acre shy of their goal.

Everyone has worked hard, but the day is far from over as they also have assignments at the barn until quitting time. They wash equipment, and do general maintenance or whatever needs to be done.

This style of farming is not all that different from the early days of the Kentucky pioneers when crops were grown to ensure survival and self-sufficiency. The labor force in those early days depended mostly upon family members.

Today, the modern equipment, the enhanced seed varieties, and the use of migrant workers have changed farming substantially, but for families like the Smiths, it remains a labor of love.

Women and girls were included in every aspect of the farm work. Most all women oversaw a garden large enough to feed the family.

Often the cultural norms of a community dictated whether women would participate in producing the tobacco crop. From pulling seedlings from the plant bed, setting the plants, hoeing, and suckering, to grading and stripping the leaves, girls and women were often included in this difficult and dirty work.[74]

"From the time that people settled in this area, between 1810 and 1830, those who owned slaves brought them with them," William Turner said. "Another great source of labor for the production of dark and burley in this region was based upon the tenant system. The sharecropper or tenant replaced the slave labor system after emancipation.

"By and large, farmers during the nineteenth century depended upon their children for labor. We know that a couple having anywhere from eight to twelve or fourteen children was common. Those children were pressed first into the knowledge, and second, the labor of producing the cash crop. This practice continued into the 1920s and '30s."[73]

Freshly set tobacco plants in the western Kentucky Black Patch. (Mitchell Richmond)

L-R Bobbie (Smith) Bryant and Shirley (Chilcutt) Smith take food to the field in the 1980s. (Smith family)

Geneva (Brewer) Smith with grandson Josh Smith prepares to set tobacco. (Smith family)

Lois (Robinson) Brewer, grandmother to Billy Smith, 1892-1975 (Smith family)

Even though it was often not socially acceptable for women to work in the fields, a family's economic situation made it necessary. As technology improved and machines made the labor less intensive, farm women began to assist only in times of real need.[75]

Billy Smith remembered his grandmother, Lois Brewer, helping mostly when her husband was running behind. "She would pull plants or drop them for others to set. It didn't happen often, but if it weren't too cold, and Papa would build a fire to keep her warm, she'd help with stripping."[76]

Billy's sister, Bettie Smith Stoll, who is seven years younger, remembered their grandmother differently. "No, I don't remember her doing any 'men's work' at all. She did her vegetable garden [freezing and canning], tended her chickens, quilted, sewed, cooked, and cleaned house. As time went by though, things changed for women. Mother did all the tobacco tasks, in the field and in the barn. I did, too. I helped set, hoe, sucker, and strip tobacco."[77]

In addition to working in the tobacco patch, the women also prepared all the food for the workers. In the Black Patch, the noon meal is usually called dinner, and "feeding the hands" refers to serving the noon meal out in the field. Women rang an iron dinner bell outside the house when it was time for the men to come in from the fields for a meal. Or, if they were working in a field too far from the house, the farm wife took the food to the field for the workers.[78]

Women played a significant role in supporting the family through the secondary businesses of the family farm: fruit, butter, and egg production. Country stores and city businesses accepted eggs, butter, and chickens in payment for goods and services. Local historians note that the egg was a significant rival to the silver dollar in the early days.[79]

Mama Brewer and her chickens (Smith family)

Hal Smith's Groceries and Meats, a country store in Mayfield, Graves County, Kentucky. (Smith family)

Tobacco grows throughout the spring and summer months. (Mitchell Richmond)

A Key Partner: The Local Bank

Local bankers have always been invaluable to farmers in areas as remote as western Kentucky. Far from the state capital and most big cities, the farmer and the banker depended on each other.

William T. Turner described the traditional relationship of tobacco farmer and banker. "Most of the farmers that came into this western Kentucky area lived on a year-by-year subsistence. If they were not able to get a nearby farmer or a family member to underwrite them, they'd have to go to the bank.

"The banker took into consideration what type of reputation the farmer had. 'What kind of young man is he? Is he reliable? Can we trust him?'

"They take the leap, loan the money, then watch him and see how he farms.

Planters Bank of Hopkinsville in 1925, was located on the northeast corner of 8th and Main Streets. (William T. Turner)

Bank of Hopkinsville in 1890, was located on the southeast corner of 7th and Main Streets. (William T. Turner)

First National Bank in 1922, was located at 5th and Main Streets in Murray, Kentucky. (Murray Main Street)

Bank of Murray in 1922, was located at 4th and Main Streets in Murray, Kentucky. (Murray Main Street)

City Bank and Trust of Hopkinsville was located on the northeast corner of 7th and Main. (William T. Turner)

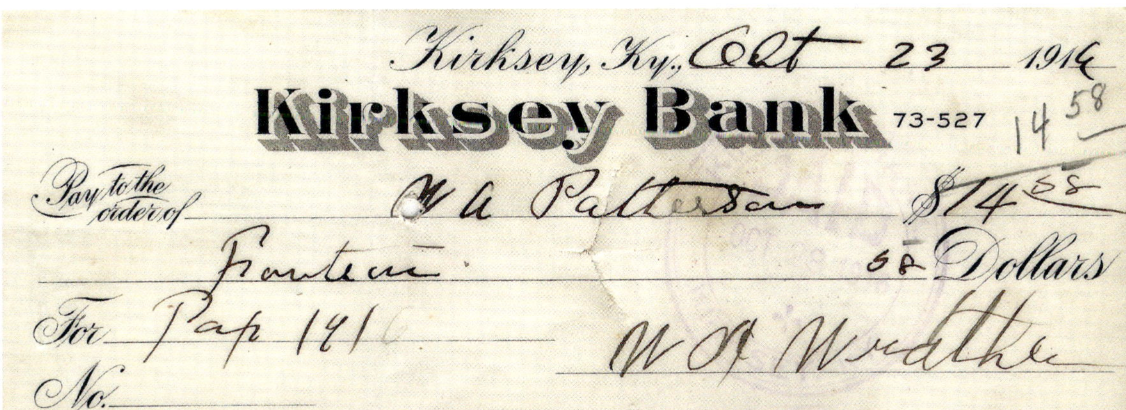

Kirksey Bank note dated October 23, 1916. The Kirksey Bank in Calloway County was organized in 1910 when stockholders pledged $15,000 for stock and a 20 x 40-foot brick building. (Smith family)

Farmers with a one-row tobacco setter in Calloway County in 1957. (Murray State University, Pogue Special Collections.)

"When a farmer goes to the bank, he presents a certain image; he's built a reputation. As the lender, you have a degree of trust in that farmer, based upon the individual's past reputation. When the farmer goes to the banker to borrow money, he has no idea what the weather, black shank, army worms, crickets, or grasshoppers might do to his crop.

"So the banker really has to take the farmer at his word and the trust he has in him as a farmer, but also faith that the good Lord will send a good crop year so he'll get his money back."[80]

An unidentified loan officer and customer discuss financial concerns at Peoples Bank of Murray. (Murray State University, Pogue Special Collections)

First City Bank of Hopkinsville in the 1940s, was located at the southwest corner of 9th and Main Streets. (William T. Turner)

Christian County Historian William T. Turner (foreground) provides items for a time capsule at the new First City Bank building in Hopkinsville. Turner is flanked on his left by Raymond McKinney, chairman of the board, and to the right, Glen Babb, president of First City Bank, on January 1, 1980. (William T. Turner)

As a farmer himself and a longtime resident of the area, H. Glen Doran had a unique understanding of farm life and knew what it took to succeed in the business. (Doran was the retired chairperson of the board of Peoples Bank of Murray, which he managed for fifty-five years. He died in November 2012.)[81]

Doran helped Billy and Billy Dale Smith and many other young farmers in the area buy their first calf or plant their cash crops.

"The tobacco end of banking was significant," he explained. "Tobacco was the money crop for this area. It was the thing farmers paid their mortgages with or bought another farm with—their tobacco. I knew the tobacco business. I'd plowed with a mule, knew farming, and I knew farmers. I'd been in the farm business and it was helpful to me in running the bank. It was also helpful to the farmer because I knew his problems. I also understood the warehouse business; I'd also prized tobacco, been in the storage business, so I had all those facets in tobacco which I knew, and it was important to our economy."

"Back then I could start a young fellow off in farming with about $500 to $600 to buy a couple of mules and have a little crop money. He'd get his crop out, then I'd take a mortgage on his crop, then he could buy five or six cows with a small dairy. Raising that tobacco, first thing you'd know, he'd have enough to make a down payment on a farm. Then he'd pay off the farm by living off the dairy during the year. At the end of the year, he'd have three to five acres of tobacco to pay off the note on his farm. That worked real well for many, many years. I didn't have any losses to speak of using that program."

Billy Smith with his show steer in the 1950s (Smith family)

Herd of cattle at Smith Farms in 1950s (Smith family)

Boys Heifer Club in Christian County. (William T. Turner)

First City Bank, located on Fort Campbell Boulevard in Christian County. (William T. Turner)

In 1956, Hopkinsville's First City Bank opened a drive-up window for car service. (William T. Turner)

Exterior of the First City Bank with its first driveup windows. (William T. Turner)

Danny Cunningham shared his experience with financing a crop. "A lot of people look back remembering when they grew up on a farm and you could make a few hundred dollars and get by. Like my dad, you could charge what you bought at the local stores back then. But now, we spend months and months, and we're out thousands of dollars to put out a crop, and I don't think people understand that.

"In 1960, when I got out of high school, I started borrowing money. Back in the '70s and '80s, the bankers got to saying that if you don't own it, you won't get it. I don't think anyone realizes what the '80s were

Planters Bank branch was located on West 9th Street in Hopkinsville in 1951. (William T. Turner)

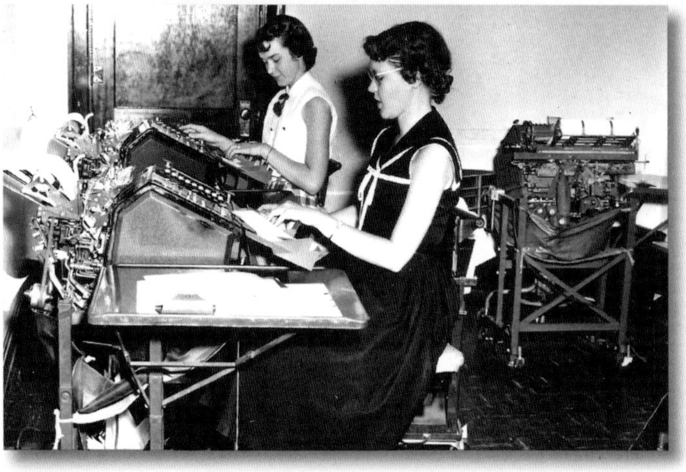

Planters Bank clerk posts checks in 1953. (William T. Turner)

Newly remodeled Planters Bank of Hopkinsville in 1956. (William T. Turner)

Planters Bank of Hopkinsville's newly installed 24-hour depository in 1974. (William T. Turner)

like to survive, as the banks didn't want to loan farmers much money. Farmers were going broke. The banks got scared and I even had to go elsewhere. It was just the idea if the whole farming economy got bad enough, like any business, they couldn't keep loaning money.

"I've had wonderful relationships with all my bankers, and I still do. I borrow lots of money. The lenders have gotten more farmer friendly because they understand it better now, and what it costs to put out a crop. I spend about $300 [per acre] on a corn crop just to buy seed, fertilizer, and chemicals. You multiply that by 2,400 acres, that's a lot of money.

"Our lenders today know when a crop is bad, why a cost is there. He knows if we're depending upon some insurance. He knows it's going to be a short payoff or that we may have to run something over into next year. They understand now what we're dealing with, that we're not out here with a couple of milk cows and three or four acres of tobacco.

"I borrowed $100,000 a few years ago, and my dad about had a fit. He had come through the Depression and didn't believe in borrowing money. He said, 'Boy, you'll never pay that back.' So, that's the difference in how it was when I grew up and what we're doing today. Today, it takes millions of dollars to operate a farm. Some of these boys that are farming 18, 20, 30,000 acres, it's just unimaginable how much money they have to borrow to operate."[82]

JohnMichael Puckett runs a much smaller farm operation. He said, "You can ask any of my friends, I'm probably the tightest person you'll ever meet. I'm kind of cheap. But that's the way I got to where I didn't have to borrow money.

"I bought my truck with one check, no big deal. Bought my tractor outright, bought a tobacco barn, no payments until I was twenty years old. That's when I got to thinking about buying a combine. I got prices and it wasn't going to be that bad. I went to a bank and they laughed at me. They said, 'You're twenty years old and have no credit—no, we're not going to loan you any money.' So I said fine, and I walked out of that bank and went to another one.

"I talked to a boy at the other bank that I'd known forever; he was two or three years older than me and lives in Marshall County. I told him I needed a loan. He asked how much I needed, and I told him I wanted to buy a combine and he said, 'Oh, about $500,000?' And I said, 'No sir, I want to buy a used one.' And he said, 'Well, however much you want, just sit down there.'"[83]

JohnMichael Puckett during an interview for the 2013 documentary, *Farming in the Black Patch*. (Bobbie Bryant)

Rob Ed Parrish combines milo at Smith Farms. (Bill Bryant)

Grain is unloaded at Smith Farms. (Bill Bryant)

Shelling corn in Calloway County
(Bill Bryant)

Tractor and disk ready for the field (Bill Bryant)

Equipment shed at Smith Farms (Bill Bryant)

The Growing Season

The tobacco is growing, and you can already begin to see the unique color and shape common to the dark variety. Farmers cross their fingers that the harvest will come without experiencing worms, wind, hailstorms, or the dreaded black shank.

"We have to apply a preventive fungicide before we have a problem," Billy Dale says. "A grower needs to know the signs and symptoms of all the tobacco diseases. Things like the temperature, moisture, air movement, and equipment sanitation, or even infested crop debris, all these things can cause problems. You've got to understand why, how, and when they occur, and know what to do to manage the diseases. As the crop is growing, we'll scout the fields frequently and look for any disease. If a disease is found and is serious enough, we might want to treat it with more fungicide."

Weather dictates the next course of action—too much rain will create all manner of problems. Too little and irrigation will be needed.

The landscape takes on a totally different look, and the sight of corn and soybeans growing in the fields is a reassuring sight for the farmer, a deeply satisfying reward after months of planning and hard work.

But the pleasure is momentary. As the season moves forward, the list of things to do for each crop grows longer.

The first tobacco crop of the season at Carraway family Farms in Calloway County (Carraway Farms)

Corn is a native plant to Kentucky, domesticated over thousands of years and shown to early pioneers by the Chickasaw Indians who inhabited the Black Patch region. (Mitchell Richmond)

Hot and humid conditions often call for irrigation during the summer. (Smith family)

Left: Soybeans at Smith Farms (Bill Bryant)

Soybeans growing at Smith Farms, with Josh Smith's tobacco barns waiting for the first crop of tobacco (Bill Bryant)

Water flows through the rows of tobacco (Smith family)

Josh Smith hauls water to the field to irrigate tobacco. (Smith family)

Workers at Smith Farms lay hose to take much-needed water to the tobacco crop. (Smith family)

Irrigation system at Carraway Family Farms (Carraway Farms)

Tobacco crop gets water from the irrigation system at Smith Farms. (Smith family)

In the tobacco fields, a "side dressing" is applied to the young plants. This special fertilizer ensures that plants get the nutrients they need. Experienced farmers know healthy plants are better able to fight off diseases; this practice can also reduce the total amount of fertilizer used by placing it close to the rows instead of scattering it over the entire field.

By the middle of June, the farmers feel somewhat confident as their crops thrive, but they don't relax for long. Darkening skies threaten hailstorms—and the daily gambles continue.

Only a few months remain in the growing season. Twenty-seven acres of tobacco have been set and the time is ripe to "top" the plants to prevent destructive suckers.

Plants flower to produce seeds. Removing the flower from the plant redirects nutrients into making bigger and thicker leaves instead of seeds.

A field of tobacco with suckers at Smith Farms (Smith family)

Billy Dale Smith checks out sucker problems at Smith Farms. (Smith family)

Workers at Lowe Farms go row by row to break off the tops of tobacco and apply chemical. (Lowe Farms)

"My ancestors had to fight the insects the entire time the tobacco was in the field," Billy says. "The tobacco worm was a pest until the tobacco was put in the barns and fires built to cure the tobacco. As the fires were started and smoke went up into the barn of hanging tobacco, the worms would start falling out as the smoke killed them.

"In the old days, you had to break out the suckers by hand. Most tobacco will put out a second sucker after the first one is broken out, so back then, they had to sucker the plant two times. Suckering tobacco was a back-breaking job. You had to bend over the plant and use your hands and fingers to break out the suckers, being careful not break the leaves."

Jose Luis Hernandez Garcia at Lowe Farms applies chemical oil directly on the suckers to stop their growth. (Lowe Farms)

Workers at Smith Farms apply chemical directly to suckers. (Smith family)

Dark clouds and torrential rain appear in the distance. (Mitchell Richmond)

While rain is welcomed during the summer months, storms can wreak havoc on crops in the field. (Cunningham Farms)

Billy Dale continues, "Today we oil the tobacco with a chemical or a growth regulator to either burn the suckers off, slow them down, or stunt them."[84]

Removing the suckers is still a labor-intensive job done by hand. The workers walk through every row, removing the flowers and suckers from the plants. Should it rain, the suckers become a serious issue. So everyone hopes for sunshine.

The weather continues to dictate work in other ways. Billy Dale has eight acres of tobacco ready to top and another four ready to cut. A tropical storm might hit the Gulf of Mexico and severe rains may be two to three days away.

Does he leave the workers in the field topping or does he cut? He knows he's got to get the early crop in the barn, get it cured, stripped, and shipped before the end of September to make room for the late crop. Knowing every minute counts, the men double their efforts. They cut four acres in two days.

The entire tobacco plant is cut close to the ground using a tobacco knife, which is shaped much like a tomahawk. The plant is then spiked and pushed onto a tobacco stick. A tobacco stick will hold five or six plants. The sticks are placed on a scaffold wagon, and left to wilt in the field for several days before being taken to a barn to cure.

Jose Felix Zamorano at Lowe Farms begins the process of cutting tobacco. (Lowe Farms)

Tobacco is cut and left in the field to wilt. (Mitchell Richmond)

Workers drop tobacco sticks at Smith Farms. (Smith family)

Cut tobacco is ready for the scaffold wagon. (Mitchell Richmond)

When ready to be harvested—or housed—each stick of tobacco is handed up from a worker on the wagon to another who is straddling beams or poles running the length of the barn. Tobacco barns typically have centrally located doors with air vents or other devices to control the amount of air and moisture around the tobacco as it hangs.

Once it is housed in the barns, the tobacco air-cures for three to five days. After that, it is time to build the fires in the barns, a crucial phase in raising dark-fired tobacco.

To get the fires going, Billy Dale uses a mixture of wood sawdust and slabs, including the wood chips and limbs from the ice storm earlier in the year. In a half day, the team builds and sets fourteen beds of fires per barn. Once lit, the fires will smolder for about a week.

Servando Pineda loads tobacco onto scaffold wagons at Smith Farms. (Smith family)

Luis Tapia and Bernardino Ruiz load sticks of tobacco onto scaffold wagons at Smith Farms. (Smith family)

Preston Carraway, son of Craig and Joanna Carraway, stands in a field of cut tobacco. (Carraway Farms)

Sayler Lowe and Cesar Contreras at Lowe Farms place tobacco onto sticks, ready for the curing barn. (Lowe Farms)

Workers at Smith Farms load tobacco onto scaffold wagons. (Bill Bryant)

Workers at Smith Farms load tobacco onto scaffold wagons. (Bill Bryant)

The Cure

As the sun sets in the distance, a thin column of smoke lingers above the Smith family tobacco barns. To the casual observer, it may appear the barns are on fire. In fact, it is not uncommon for alarmed tourists to knock on a farmer's door in Calloway County to alert him to the potential disaster.

"Depending on how excited the person is, and usually they are, I will always go and make sure the barns are okay," Billy Dale says. "Knock on wood, I have never lost a barn to fire, but I have had other problems such as wind damage, scorched tobacco, house burn, and sweated tobacco. I know what I must do to cure the tobacco in the barn, but I also know that if I misjudge the conditions in the barn I can damage or ruin the crop. The good tobacco farmers learn from the mistakes they make and move on. They try to remember what happened and try not to repeat it, or figure out what has to be done and when at the precise time.

"Depending on what kind of shape the tobacco is, we want it to go through a yellowing process at the beginning, but we'll start the fires actually before it turns yellow, and the reason we are doing that is we are trying to get some heat and some air movement to keep it from sweating in the barn.

Smoking barn at Carraway Family Farms
(Bill Bryant)

Smoking barns in Christian County (William T. Turner)

Tobacco barns in Calloway County (Deana Wright)

Smoking barn in the Black Patch region (Dr. Andy Bailey)

Smoking barn at Smith Farms
(Bill Bryant)

Above: Tobacco barns in Calloway County (Deana Wright)

"In these big barns, we may have up to fourteen beds of fire in each one. That consists of one semi-trailer load of sawdust and five to six bundles of wood slabs. We'll start the fires and the fires will gradually get hotter and hotter over a period of days after they get started burning. It will depend on how hot we want it to get; we can build one fire, two fires, three fires, or four to a bed. It will usually burn for about a week and, like I said, we will have three to four different fires in here. The first one pretty much sets the color, the second one will kill the stalk, and the third fire will put the finish on it. Sometimes we need to fire it a fourth time to help get some more finish on the tobacco with that distinctive aroma."

Billy Dale Smith moves tobacco into the barn. (Smith family)

Francisco Javier Rojas Canales (in the straw hat) is at the top of the barn with Heriberto Rodriguez, at Carraway Family Farms. (Carraway Farms)

Heriberto Rodriguez places sticks of tobacco in the top of a tobacco barn at Carraway Family Farms. (Carraway Farms)

Tobacco is run into the barn at Smith Farms. (Smith family)

Worker on a farm in Christian County in the top tier of the tobacco barn. (William T. Turner)

Tobacco hung in a barn to cure in Christian County. (William T. Turner)

Workers hang tobacco at Smith Farms. (Bill Bryant)

Farmers refer to tobacco that is moist enough to keep the leaves from crumbling as being "in order." H. Glen Doran described the curing process when tobacco comes in order. "Tobacco is dry when you fire it. You let the moisture come along—open the barn doors and get the tobacco moist so you can handle it without breaking it up when you take it off the stalk to strip it. A lot of people used thermometers so they'd know what they were doing. You'd do that for several days and see what color you'd get. If you weren't getting the color you wanted, you'd quit and hope for a rainy day and you'd fire it again, hoping to get the color and finish you wanted."[85]

"Firing was a lot different when I was a kid," Danny Cunningham says. "I've seen my dad back up in the corner of a barn and sit for three, four, or five hours at a time, to make sure the fires didn't get too hot, didn't sweat. Now we build the fires up, shut the doors, and go on to the next one. We're liable to build fires in five or six barns in the morning, so we don't have time to watch the barns like my dad did. My dad would probably turn over in his grave to see me build a barn fire the way I do it versus how he used to do it."

"There are a whole lot of different tobacco growers in western Kentucky," noted JohnMichael Puckett. "And nobody does anything exactly the same. It's still the same basics. I mean, you go in, you build your first fire, and you get your color through. After the color comes through, you build your second fire a little hotter and you cook the sap out of the stems and preferably out of the stalks. And the rest of your fires are just going for smoke. And the more smoke you put on it, I think, to an extent, the better it will look."

Tobacco hangs in a barn. (Dr. Andy Bailey)

Billy Dale says, "You've got the vents on the bottom and vents on the top and you control the environment inside the barn by using your ventilators either at the top or the bottom to control the humidity and the firing process inside the barn. All barns have a personality, just like each one of us do. And after you deal with them, you learn their personalities. In these old barns, we fired for years and put a crop in them, and you never could really control the environment inside of them to get the product out or the finish of the tobacco like you want it to be finished."

Workers at Carraway Family Farms move sawdust into the barn, preparing for firing process. (Carraway Farms)

Jose Manuel Valdez pushes the wheelbarrow of sawdust as Jose Santos Lopez and Ruben Mancera drop wood at Carraway Family Farms. (Carraway Farms)

Dario Sandoval Martinez (left), Juan Jose Michel (holding wood slab) Raul Alexis Benavides (far right) and Jose Alfredo Lopez (center back) arrange slabs and sawdust at Carraway Family Farms. (Carraway Farms)

Workers at Smith farms arrange sawdust in preparation for firing process. (Smith family)

Jose Esteban Zuniga with his back to the camera, Antonio Luna and Orlando Guzman Estrada at Carraway Farm, spreading sawdust in preparation for firing process. (Carraway Farms)

Above: Barn at Carraway Family Farms is ready for fires to cure the tobacco. (Carraway Farms)

Wood slabs are delivered to Lowe Farms by tractor trailer. (Lowe Farms)

Workers use the forklift to move slabs into the barn in preparation for the firing process. (Smith family)

Sometimes tobacco barns have burned down during the curing process. Scott Lowe shared a personal story. "The second year of raising a tobacco crop, I had a barn go up in flames in the middle of the night. My wife was pregnant with our first daughter. We were young and dumb with no tobacco insurance and no fire insurance, and so that was a big blow for us. Nights like that make you wonder why you're a tobacco farmer. But, there's been more good years than bad and tobacco has been really good to us."[86]

The process of growing a tobacco crop, understanding the feel, the look, the smell, is something that is learned from experience. It is as much an art form as science.

Hickory wood slabs lie against the side of the barn at Smith Farms. (Smith family)

Smoke from the curing barn seeps through the open door. (Mitchell Richmond)

Hickory wood is in place for setting fires at Smith Farms. (Smith family)

Kyle Tracy sets a fire to begin curing tobacco at Smith Farms. (Smith family)

Burley hangs in the open shed to air-cure at Smith Farms. (Bill Bryant)

Right: Burley tobacco is covered in canvas to protect it from moisture. (Bill Bryant)

Burley hangs on structures in a field at Smith Farms. (Bill Bryant)

Smoking barns at dusk at Smith Farms (Smith family)

Smoking barn at the Grundy Falwell farm in Calloway County (Deana Wright)

The Finishing Touches

It's been a hard year, but Billy Dale is confident he'll have a season to be proud of. Still, he can't relax, starting at four thirty every morning to check the weather, make plans, make adjustments—sometimes every hour.

It's September and there are still several acres to cut and house. But soon the first and second barns are stripped and stored away, ready for market. There are ten acres still to be stripped and taken to the warehouses so the workers can return to their families in Mexico in time for Christmas. If the tobacco isn't stripped, no one goes home early.

The eight men strip an acre a day, engaging in yet another difficult and labor-intensive process. The workers form a sort of assembly line to pull the leaves off the stalks by hand. The color and thickness of the leaves determine what category they go in. This process requires the stripper to know good leaves from the not-so-good. In years past, farmers took great pride in this skill.[87] The leaves would be sorted by size or color. When the farmer had a handful of leaves, he tied them in a bundle, creating what was called a "hand" of tobacco. In those days, many grades of tobacco went to market where they were stacked on baskets to be bid on separately.

Double crop of tobacco at Smith Farms
(Bill Bryant)

Hauling tobacco to the barn at Smith Farms (Bill Bryant)

Tyler Boggess takes tobacco down from the barn at Smith Farms. (Smith family)

Jose Roberto Barrios at Carraway Family Farms strips tobacco leaves from the plant. (Carraway Farms)

A stripping line is well underway at Carraway Family Farms. (Carraway Farms)

Unidentified men strip leaves from tobacco plants and tie them into hands in a Kentucky tobacco barn in 1969. (University of Kentucky Libraries, Special Collections Research Center)

Geneva (Brewer) Smith (1915–2000) helps her grandson, Billy Dale Smith, strip tobacco in the 1980s. (Smith family)

H. Glen Doran recalled the socializing aspects of the work in those days. "Used to be that when the farmer had to cut the tobacco, he would use their neighbors and swap labor. When they'd strip tobacco, the women folks would come in, and they'd have a big time talking and have a dinner, and they'd strip the tobacco without any labor costs involved."

Billy Dale Smith shared a similar story about his paternal grandparents. "When my Granny and Granddaddy Smith were living, they'd invite their retired friends to come help us strip. The younger adults would take the lugs off at the wagon, then throw the leaves on a table and stand there on concrete floors, stripping the leaves."[88]

Billy Dale's son, Josh, explained the way things have changed in the twenty-first century. "Now we've got a line of people with a conveyor belt with a chain and motor on the back. The tobacco stalk is on a stick and as it comes in, you take it off the wagon, and put it on the conveyor belt. Once it is on the belt, it starts through the stripping line. Each person in the line has a different job. At the beginning, the lugs and trash come off, leaving only the best leaves. The people in the back of the line take off the good leaves and put them in a box for shipping. The boxes weigh hundreds of pounds."[89]

Once the tobacco is stripped, the leaves are packed tightly into large cardboard boxes and loaded onto semi-tractor trailers for delivery to market. The discarded stalks are bundled and used in low-lying areas of fields around the farm to prevent soil erosion.

Everyone works frantically to stay ahead. It is important to get the tobacco stripped as quickly as possible. In a matter of days, the weather can shift, the tobacco can dry out, and additional moisture may be needed to reestablish the right conditions in the barns.

Given the incentive to finish—being home by Christmas—the men work overtime, often late into the evening. Soon the crop is done and the migrant workers leave for Mexico, but for Billy Dale, his dad, Billy, and his son, Josh, it seems as though the work never ends. They reflect for a moment on a busy and productive year, but soon turn their energies to planning the next year's crops.

Billy Dale's schedule has worked for another season. He succeeded despite ice storms, torrential rains, insects, rising production prices, and an evaporating labor force. The only remaining question is whether he's made any money. Billy Dale hopes he's covered his costs. He also hopes to get a new, perhaps bigger, contract next year.

The days grow shorter and winter is just around the corner.

Bernardino Ruiz strips leaves and packs them into boxes for market. (Smith family)

L-R: Workers at Smith Farms use their weight to press more tobacco into boxes for shipping. (Smith family)

Tyler Boggess strips tobacco at Smith Farms. (Smith Family)

Juan Sosa strips tobacco leaves from the stalk. (Smith family)

Workers at the stripping line at Smith Farms. (Smith family)

Tobacco is stripped, boxed, and ready for shipping. (Mitchell Richmond)

To Market

In early America, tobacco was marketed in 100-pound rolls. Then the cask or hogshead was introduced, ranging from 500 to 1,500 pounds. Tobacco growers would bring their tobacco to licensed warehouses, usually located by a river or the sea.[90]

The tobacco was weighed, inspected, sorted, and graded by official inspectors. The planter was given an inspection receipt or crop note. These notes were legal tender and served the same purpose as commercial paper. The planter could sell his notes to a merchant, exchange them for other products, or pay his debts.[91]

Today, the process of selling tobacco doesn't look much like it did just a few decades ago. In the 1930s, there was an auction system and some farmers sold directly to tobacco companies. When a farmer took his tobacco to market, it was generally on a flatbed wagon pulled by a team of mules or horses.

In the loose-leaf warehouse auction system, there was little the farmer could do once his crop went to market. A farmer selected which auction house he went to according to friendships and the service he received.[92]

A tobacco warehouse in Murray, Kentucky, with hogsheads full of tobacco, brought in by farmers on wagons. (Murray Main Street)

Outland Brother's Tobacco Warehouse in 1922, located in Murray (Murray Main Street)

American Snuff Company located on East 21st in Hopkinsville in the 1930s (William T. Turner)

United States Tobacco Company in Hopkinsville (William T. Turner)

"Sometime after the Depression, during the Franklin D. Roosevelt administration, the US government's farm program was created," Billy Smith said. "The program established a federal government grading system to assess tobacco quality, issuing grade cards defining different quality and price levels, and then grading each farmer's tobacco as it was readied for market.

"Each tobacco-producing region was required to form its own association, or cooperative, to buy farmers' tobacco at a guaranteed price when the commercial buyers' bids were too low during the warehouse auction or they refused to pay the government-graded price. Farmers would receive checks from the government, and the associations would process the tobacco and hold it until it could be sold to local, national, or international buyers at a profit. Tobacco that was purchased by the association, or co-op, was referred to as going to the 'pool.'"[93]

The way a farmer sells his tobacco changed dramatically in 2004, when legislation was enacted that significantly changed US tobacco policy. The Fair and Equitable Tobacco Reform Act (FETRA) was included as Title VII of the American Jobs Creation Act of 2004. Now it is imperative for farmers to contract their future crop ahead of growing, and they do so directly with tobacco companies.

This legislation is commonly referred to as the "Tobacco Buyout." The act repealed the federal tobacco price support and quota programs and disposed of existing pool stocks. It also paid tobacco quota owners and growers for their quota. The new buyout was spread over a ten-year period, with payments to end in 2014.[94]

The act removed restrictions on who could grow tobacco and how much could be produced. There were no geographic limitations placed on production and no price support levels. These changes affected laws that had been in place since 1938.

Randy Hale on forklift with tobacco, 1981 (William T. Turner)

Billy Dale Smith is satisfied with how the buyout program is working for his operation. "The buyout program has put tobacco production back into the tobacco grower's hands rather than quota owners. In the past, we didn't have enough base [acreage] or quota [pounds], so we had to reach out to other farm owners to rent ground and their base for growing tobacco. The base was so hard to get in our county, many farmers had to go south into Tennessee to rent land and/or the base, or quota. Since the buyout, the tobacco companies tell us how much to grow. We grow it and sell it directly to the tobacco companies."[95]

Danny Cunningham believes the buyout was good for farmers while it lasted. "A lot of farmers paid for their land or paid off their debts. Some of the smaller farms will probably miss it once it's gone, but it won't hurt people. We almost went broke during the 1980s, so for me and Judy, we got money that we'd never have been able to save."

"One interesting aspect or result of the tobacco buyout has been the effect on land prices," noted H. Glen Doran.[96] "One of the provisions in it was whatever they paid the farmer for the acres he had, they'd do it over a ten-year period, or he could take it to the bank, or cash it out all in one lick. But he wouldn't have to pay any income tax on that money if he'd put it back into a farming operation or back into land.

"So it was a big incentive to buy land. Instead of land that was selling for $700 or $800 an acre, now it sells for $3,000 or $4,000 an acre, which is great for a fella that owned a bunch of land. But what it does to the young farmer coming along, it means it is almost impossible for him to start out in farming any more. For those young boys that came in before we got out of the bank that wanted to get into farming, I'd tell them, 'Now there are two ways to start farming. One way is to buy into it and the other is to inherit.'

"That was one of the results of the buyout that we did not foresee. That's a mixed blessing—great for someone who owns a bunch of land, but tough for those who want to buy land. It's also going to be tough for the fella who owns land because when he dies, the government is going to appraise the land at this high figure, and [his heirs will] have a tough time with inheritance tax."

Southwestern Tobacco Warehouse in Hopkinsville (William T. Turner)

Conwood Corporation Snuff Division (William T. Turner)

A Closing Note

The reasons people still grow tobacco are sometimes more cultural than economic. For some tobacco farmers, it is a long-ingrained habit, a tradition going back generations, bonding families to the plant, to their land, and to each other.

For tobacco farm families, life is punctuated by the rhythms of cultivation: setting, plowing, topping, spraying, cutting, curing, stripping, and marketing mark the passage of time as surely as holidays in the cycle of a year.

But that's life on the farm, a cycle that has endured for centuries and will continue as long as a love for the land remains a family tradition.

Tobacco grows another year at Smith Farms. (Smith family)

A close-up view of tobacco plants at Smith Farms. (Bill Bryant)

Billy and Shirley Smith walk the grounds at Smith Farms. (Michael Breeding)

A twenty-first-century farmer, Logan Smith, is proud of his gardening abilities. (Smith family)

Josh, Logan, and Carter Smith are at work on Smith Farms. (Smith family)

A long work day is over for Carter Smith at Smith Farms. (Smith family)

Signs of the past linger in Calloway County. (Bobbie Bryant)

An old plow shows the ways of our ancestors. (Bobbie Bryant)

A corn crib in Calloway County
(Bill Bryant)

March flowers announce the arrival of spring at Smith Farms. (Bill Bryant)

A fall landscape (Betsy Bryant)

Fall arrives at Smith Farms. (Smith family)

Another winter at Smith Farms. (Smith family)

Richard Duke's tobacco barn in Calloway County. (Deana Wright)

A road leads to the field. (Bill Bryant)

A tobacco barn at Josh Smith's.
(Bill Bryant)

Afterword

The federal tobacco program, consisting of minimum price levels, guaranteed markets, and production quotas, provided tobacco growers with some protection from the market power of the large tobacco companies. During most of the twentieth century, it was arguably the most effective federal farm policy program originating from President Roosevelt's New Deal ag programs in the 1930s. However, after more than sixty years of existence, the federal tobacco program began to unravel during the 1980s and 1990s. A series of policy adjustments during this time frame provided some temporary relief, but were eventually ineffective in improving the price competitiveness of US tobaccos and reducing the cost structure for tobacco growers. Declining demand caused production quota levels to decline rapidly during the late 1990s and early 2000s, and tobacco grower profits were reduced significantly. Tobacco quota owners feared that Congress would eliminate the program without compensation for their assets, while tobacco growers feared lower-priced foreign leaf and escalating marketing assessments would continue to take away profitable production opportunities.

Close-up view of dark tobacco (Bill Bryant)

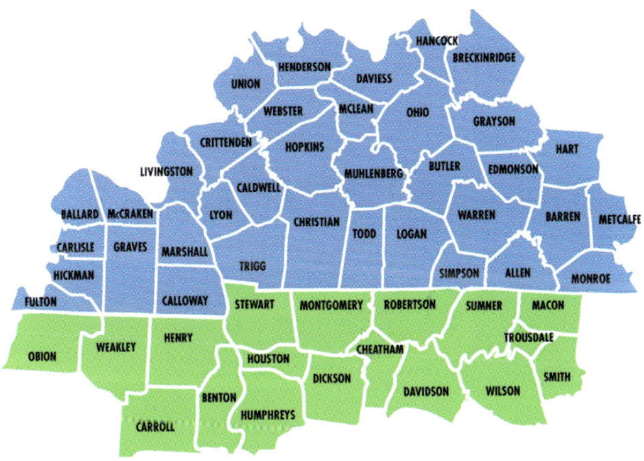

1930s map of the counties included in the Black Patch region of Kentucky and Tennessee.

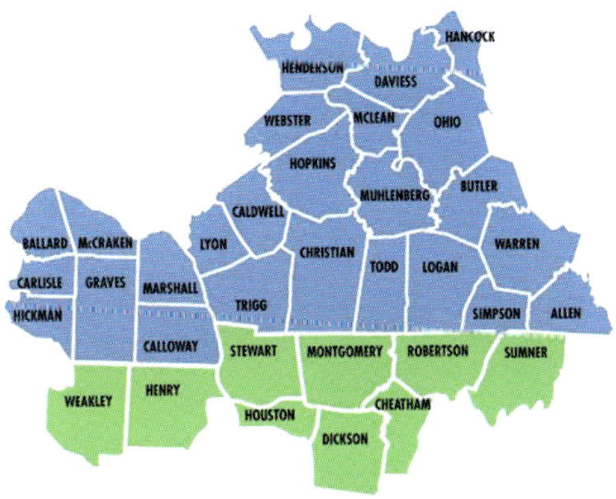

2004 map of the counties included in the Black Patch region of Kentucky and Tennessee

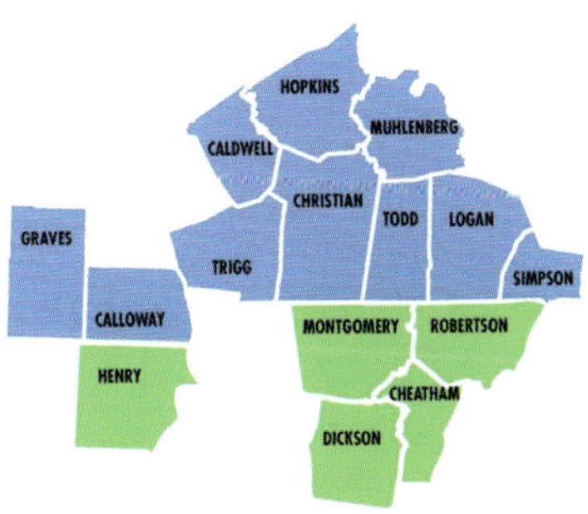

2014 map of the counties included in the Black Patch region of Kentucky and Tennessee

Burley tobacco grows during the summer at Carraway Family Farms. (Carraway Farms)

Collectively, tobacco quota owners, growers, farm and health organizations, and tobacco companies lobbied Congress for a program buyout during the 1990s and early 2000s, which, unlike other taxpayer-funded government farm programs, would be financed by assessments on US tobacco companies based on the sale of tobacco products in the domestic market. Finally in 2004, the buyout became reality as quota owners received compensation for the elimination of their quota assets, growers received compensation to diversify away from tobacco or adjust to selling tobacco in a free market, tobacco companies could purchase US leaf at lower prices, and health groups eventually were rewarded with increased federal regulation of tobacco products. When the law passed, I said:

> After more than a decade of debate, the tobacco buyout will become reality with the president's signature on the American Jobs Creation Act of 2004. The tobacco quota buyout is probably the most significant and far-reaching piece of agricultural policy legislation for Kentucky farmers and rural communities since the development of the federal tobacco program in the 1930s. While the buyout will inject nearly $2.5 billion into Kentucky's local and rural economies over the next ten years, it will undoubtedly change the landscape of the Kentucky agricultural economy forever.

Servando Pineda (foreground) and Bernardino Ruiz plow tobacco the old-fashioned way, with mules and a walk-behind plow. (Bobbie Bryant)

Close-up view of tobacco as it cures. (Dr. Andy Bailey)

Kyle Tracy drives the tractor as Tyler Boggess, Juan Sosa, and Luis Tapia apply chemical to suckers on tobacco plants. (Smith family)

Luis Tapia collects pollen from burley plants for cross pollination at Smith Farms. (Smith family)

Tobacco cures in the Black Patch (Dr. Andy Bailey)

The tobacco buyout certainly transformed Kentucky agriculture, resulting in the greatest structural change in any tobacco-producing state. The number of farms growing tobacco in the Commonwealth declined from around 60,000 in the early 1990s to fewer than 5,000 by 2012, as most previous quota owners and growers retired or decided to produce other crops. Tobacco production shifted out of eastern and central Kentucky to larger, lower-cost-of-production farms in western Kentucky. The average size of tobacco acreage per farm increased from fewer than five acres prior to the buyout to around twenty acres by 2012, with some farms growing fifty to one hundred or more acres. More than 95 percent of the crop was marketed through production contracts with individual tobacco companies, leaving only a few auction markets surviving to purchase non-contract leaf. Lower prices and production levels resulted in Kentucky's tobacco income initially falling from its peak of more than $900 million in the late 1990s to around $300 million right after the buyout, before rebounding to around $400 million in recent years. Farmers diversified into other crops such as beef cattle, grains, vegetables, and other ag enterprises, which enabled Kentucky farm income to actually grow despite the large loss of tobacco income. Tobacco's share of the Kentucky ag economy dwindled from its historical level of around one-quarter to one-third of total Kentucky ag

Grain bins at Smith Farms (Bill Bryant)

Soybeans grow at Josh Smith's farm. (Bill Bryant)

sales to less than 10 percent. Despite a multitude of challenges and declining trends facing the tobacco industry, many farms that remained in the industry for the first decade after the buyout actually experienced increased production opportunities amidst growing demand for dark tobacco for increasing smokeless tobacco product sales, and the need for more burley tobacco induced by the mass exodus of US growers, tight global supplies, and improved competitive prices for US leaf. However, labor challenges and aging infrastructure (barns and equipment) constrained additional growth for Kentucky and US tobacco farms.

The future of the industry one decade after the ending of the federal tobacco program remains very much in doubt. Although the outlook for dark tobacco appears favorable with a stable to growing smokeless tobacco product market, taxes, health concerns, and international competition continue to erode markets for Kentucky burley with slumping domestic and global cigarette sales. Future US and global regulations on the manufacturing of tobacco products and immigration reform create additional uncertainties for growers. Plus an emerging electronic cigarette/vaping market, currently using virtually zero US tobacco, puts future demand for the crop in jeopardy as tobacco companies and consumers and some health advocates promote sales of these non-combustible products versus cigarettes. Collectively, these factors will likely result in reduced demand for tobacco leaf and induce future consolidation of the number of farms growing this crop. The likely survivors will be the lowest-cost-of-production farms that produce the highest-quality leaf and are willing to adapt to the increasing demands of tobacco companies, government agencies, and consumers.

–Dr. William M. Snell
University of Kentucky
Department of Agriculture Economics

William M. Snell, Ph. D.

Sending white corn to the grain bins in Calloway County (Bill Bryant)

Combining wheat in Calloway County (Bill Bryant)

Wheat field in the Black Patch
(Mitchell Richmond)

Field of milo (Bill Bryant)

Footnotes & Endnotes

1 W. F. Axton, *Tobacco and Kentucky* (Lexington, KY: University Press of Kentucky, 1975), 1.
2 James O. Nall, *The Tobacco Night Riders of Kentucky and Tennessee* (Kuttawa, KY: McClanahan Publishing House, 1991), 3.
3 Thomas D. Clark, *Agrarian Kentucky* (Lexington, KY: University Press of Kentucky, 1977), viii.
4 Ibid., 11.
5 Bobbie Smith Bryant, *Forty Acres and a Red Belly Ford: The Smith Family of Calloway County* (Lexington, KY: Clark Publishing, 2010), 14.
6 W. F. Axton, *Tobacco and Kentucky*, 6.
7 Marcus, "History of Tobacco and Pipe Smoking, Part I" on E. A. Carey (Europe) Ltd. website, http://www.eacarey.co.uk.
8 Axton, *Tobacco and Kentucky*, 8.
9 William Elsey Connelley and E. M. Coulter, *History of Kentucky* (Chicago, IL: American Historical Society, 1922), 1162.
10 Gene Borio, "The Tobacco Timeline 1993-2011," on Tobacco.org website, http://archive.tobacco.org/resources/history/Tobacco_History.html. Accessed January 19, 2013.
11 Gene Borio, "History of Tobacco, Part 1," on History Net website, http://www.historian.org/bysubject/tobacco1.htm, accessed January 19, 2013.
12 Ibid. Also see Connelley and Coulter, *History of Kentucky*, 1162
13 Nall, *Tobacco Night Riders*, 1.
14 "Spain still lighting up despite new tobacco laws," ThinkSpain website, April 18, 2006, http://www.thinkspain.com/news-spain/10943.
15 Borio, "History of Tobacco," History Net website.
16 Ibid. *Also see* Nall, *Tobacco Night Riders,* 1
17 Borio, "History of Tobacco," History Net website.
18 Clark, *Agrarian Kentucky*, 6.
19 Nall, *Tobacco Night Riders*, 2.
20 Axton, *Tobacco and Kentucky*, 82.
21 Ibid., 87.
22 Lowell H. Harrison and James C. Klotter, *A New History of Kentucky* (Lexington, KY: University Press of Kentucky, 1997), 258.
23 Ibid., 257.
24 Tracy Campbell, *Politics of Despair* (Lexington, KY: University Press of Kentucky, 1993), 44.
25 Ibid., 38–9.
26 Ibid., 46.
27 *Farming in the Black Patch* (Lexington, KY: Michael Breeding Media, 2012).
28 William T. Turner, interview with author, September 2012.
29 Justice Bill Cunningham, interview with author, September 2012.
30 Axton, *Tobacco and Kentucky*, 88.
31 Ibid., 91.
32 Justice Bill Cunningham, interview with author, September 2012.
33 Axton, *Tobacco and Kentucky*, 91.
34 Campbell, *Politics of Despair*, 82.
35 Justice Bill Cunningham, interview with author, September 2012.
36 Bill Cunningham, *On Bended Knees: The Night Rider Story* (Nashville, TN: McClanahan Publishing House, 1983), 141.
37 Also see Axton, *Tobacco and Kentucky*, 92.
38 Justice Bill Cunningham, interview with author, September 2012.
39 Axton, *Tobacco and Kentucky*, 9.
40 Cunningham, *On Bended Knees*, 115-16.
41 Axton, *Tobacco and Kentucky*, 94.
42 Justice Bill Cunningham, interview with author, September 2012.

43 "Number of Farms, Average Size of Farm and Land in Farms, Kentucky 1980-2009," United States Department of Agriculture National Agriculture Statistics Service website, http://www.nass.usda.gov/Statistics_by_State/Kentucky/index.asp, accessed January 20, 2013.

44 Thomas D. Clark, Lowell H. Harrison, and James C. Klotter, *The Kentucky Encyclopedia* (Lexington: KY: University Press of Kentucky, 1992), 611.

45 William T. Turner, interview with author, September 2012.

46 Kerby and Dorothy Jennings, *The Story of Calloway County, 1822-1976* (Murray, KY: Murray Democrat Publishing Co., 1980), 1.

47 Ibid., 17.

48 Billy Dale Smith, interview with author, February 25, 2010.

49 Scott Lowe, interview with author, September 2012.

50 University of Kentucky College of Agriculture, Labor Education, accessed March 23, 2013, http://www.ca.uky.edu/agecon/index.php?p=271.

51 Billy Dale Smith, interview with author, February 25, 2010.

52 Shea Lowe, *Hands in the Dirt, Hearts at Work* blog, accessed January 1, 2014, http://handsinthedirt-heartsatwork.blogspot.com/p/our-farm.html.

(Mitchell Richmond)

53 Francisco Tovar Gonzáles , interview with Meg Sumners, July 5, 2014.
54 José Jonathan Barrera Jiménez, interview with Arturo Bustamante, July 5, 2014.
55 José Luis Tapia Rodriguez, video interview, *Farming in the Black Patch*, September 9, 2012.
56 Bernardino Ruiz Cardenas, video interview, *Farming in the Black Patch*, September 9, 2012.
57 José Jonathan Barrera Jiménez, personal interview with Bustamante, July 5, 2014.
58 Bernardino Ruiz Cardenas. Interview with Josh Chambers, July 5, 2014.
59 José Luis Tapia Rodriguez, personal interview with Arturo Bustamante, July 5, 2014.
60 Francisco Tovar Gonzáles , interview with Meg Sumners, July 5, 2014.
61 Billy Smith, Jr., interview with author, December 9, 2007.
62 Billy Smith, Jr., email to author, April 8, 2013.
63 Clark, Harrison, and Klotter, *The Kentucky Encyclopedia*, 885.
64 Steve Carraway, interview with author, September 10, 2012.
65 Nall, *Tobacco Night Riders*, 4.
66 Craig Carraway, interview with author, September 10, 2012.
67 Bryant, *Forty Acres and a Red Belly Ford*, 7.
68 Billy Smith, Jr., email to author, April 8, 2013.
69 Bryant, *Forty Acres and a Red Belly Ford*, 17.
70 Billy Smith, Jr., email to author, April 8, 2013.
71 Billy Dale Smith, email to author, February 5, 2010.
72 Bryant, *Forty Acres and a Red Belly Ford*, 72.
73 William T. Turner, interview with author, September 2012.
74 Effie Marquess Carmack, *Out of the Black Patch: The Autobiography of Effie Marquess Carmack* (Logan, UT: Utah State University Press, 1999), 15.
75 Jeffery A. Duvall, "Knowing About the Tobacco: Women, Burley, and Farming in the Central Ohio River Valley," *Register of the Kentucky Historical Society* 108, no. 4 (Autumn 2010), 325.
76 William H. Smith, Jr., interview with author, March 20, 2013.
77 Betty L. Smith Stoll, email correspondence, March 20, 2013.
78 Bryant, *Forty Acres and a Red Belly Ford*, 40.
79 Ibid., 15. Also see Dorothy and Kerby Jennings, *The Story of Calloway County 1822-1976* (Murray, KY: Murray Democrat Publishing Co., 1980).
80 William T. Turner, interview with author, September 2012.
81 H. Glen Doran, interview with videographer, January 2010. He was a farmer in Lynn Grove, Kentucky, and retired chairperson of People's Bank of Murray, which he managed for fifty-five years. He died in November 2012.
82 Danny Cunningham, Calloway County farmer, interview with author, September 2012.
83 JohnMichael Puckett, Marshall County farmer, interview with author, September 2012.
84 Billy Dale Smith, email to author, February 5, 2010.
85 H. Glen Doran, interview with videographer, January 2010.
86 Scott Lowe, interview with author, September 11, 2012.
87 Clark, Harrison, and Klotter, *The Kentucky Encyclopedia*, 886.
88 Bryant, *Forty Acres and a Red Belly Ford*, 76.
89 Ibid., 77.
90 Connelley and Coulter, *History of Kentucky*, 1167.
91 Ibid.
92 Clark, Harrison, and Klotter, *The Kentucky Encyclopedia*, 886.
93 Bryant, *Forty Acres and a Red Belly Ford*, 80.
94 Kelly Tiller, Will Snell, and Blake Brown, *Tobacco Quota Buyout: Questions and Answers* (Lexington, KY: University of Kentucky Cooperative Extension, UK College of Agriculture, 2004.)
95 Billy Dale Smith, interview with Patty Ranft at *Kentucky Monthly* magazine, October 4, 2012. "Preserving the Black Patch Heritage," *Kentucky Monthly Magazine*, (November 2012), page 6.
96 H. Glen Doran, interview with videographer, January 2010.

Glossary

Base refers to the amount of acreage a farmer has under his control to grow a crop of tobacco. If an adequate amount of acreage is not available for the amount of crop a farmer has been allotted, he has to rent acres from another farm nearby.

Black Patch is the terminology used to describe the region of western Kentucky and northwestern Tennessee where dark-leaf tobacco is grown.

Black Shank is a disease that can have a disastrous effect on a tobacco crop. The disease can occur during any stage of the growing cycle and can rot the crown or root of the tobacco plant.

Burley is a type of tobacco grown and processed for cigarettes.

Cask refers to a large container or hogshead. The term specifically implies volume. Tobacco was shipped in these large casks in pioneer days as an inexpensive way to ship tobacco to market.

Chaw is another word for chewing tobacco.

Chewing tobacco is a type of smokeless tobacco, consumed by placing a small amount of dried leaves between the cheek and gum or upper lip, and chewing. Remaining juices may be spit into a nearby container.

Color of tobacco is very important during the growing cycle. The color is determined by the type of tobacco and the process used to cure it. Burley has a yellow-green color in the field and when cured or dried in the barn, it becomes a light bright color, a reddish color, or a greenish color, depending on the weather or how much time and effort the framer put into it. Dark air-cured tobacco is supposed to be a light brown, depending on the weather and the grower's ability to keep it from drying out green. Dark-fired tobacco color depends on how the tobacco is handled in the barn. The grower has to know how much fire is too much and when it is not hot enough. If it gets too hot in the barn, the tobacco will be a greenish color and not brown or dark brown, which buyers find of greater value.

Cooperatives are organized, owned, and managed by members who use their services. The primary goal for a cooperative is to make more money for its members than they could receive on their own.

Cure refers to the maturation process of the tobacco as it grows and is managed while in the barn. Properly cured tobacco is the result of a managed process and it enables the farmer to get the highest price at market. To cure tobacco means to apply heat and moisture at the appropriate times so that the leaves ripen from green to yellow and finally to brown.

Dark-fired tobacco refers to the process of smoking tobacco as it hangs in a closed barn. The use of levers and a ventilation system enables the farmer to control the humidity and obtain the proper finish on the tobacco leaves.

Dark-leaf tobacco is a heavier variety of tobacco that is cured by drying and flavoring with smoke and heat from open hickory fires within barns.

Double crop/double fill is the practice of curing two crops of tobacco in one barn during one season. This practice has increased in recent years as a way for famers to increase production and profitability. The first crop is generally set very early in May and the second crop is set in the middle of June. The farmer must cure the first crop and strip it and then cut and house the second crop in same barn.

Fair and Equitable Tobacco Reform Act became Title VII of the American Jobs Creation Act of 2004. The act is federal legislation enacted to significantly change US tobacco policy. The act repealed the federal tobacco price support and quota programs, and disposed of existing pool stocks. It also paid tobacco quota owners and growers for their quota.

Feeding the hands means to feed all the workers who are under the employ of a single farm owner. Tradition required that ample food be taken to the field in order that farmhands might have adequate sustenance to get through the long work day.

Grade cards were established through a federal government grading system to assess tobacco quality. The grade cards defined different quality and price levels, and recorded the grade of each farmer's tobacco as it was readied for market.

Grading of tobacco leaves was considered a specialty in earlier farm days. Knowing the distinctions between lugs, seconds, and leaf, was critically important when presenting the crop at market. Each grade was put into a different pile and the stripper then created a *hand* of leaves out of the same graded tobacco.

Greened (as in "greened barns") refers to tobacco that was fired too hot. The tobacco turns green and this color will not come out. Tobacco that is considered green is less desirable and will generally sell for a reduced price at market. The fires in the barns must be controlled, and farmers often use sawdust to maintain the fire at a slow burn.

Hand of tobacco describes the former way of preparing tobacco for selling. Each individual leaf of tobacco is removed from the cut stalk, and graded by size and quality. The stripper fills his hand with the leaves, and holds them at the stem. They squeeze as many as they can hold (usually eight to fourteen), then use another leaf to *tie* the hand together. The *tie leaf* is folded lengthwise, wrapped tightly around the *hand*, tucking the end of the tie leaf into the loose leaves of the hand.

Hanging tobacco is the process of placing each tobacco plant onto a tobacco stick, then loading it on a scaffold pulled by a tractor or truck. The scaffold is pulled into a barn, and each stick of tobacco is raised up by workers into the tiers of the barn where it hangs to cure.

Hoeing tobacco was necessary during colonial times to keep weeds to a minimum. In more recent times, herbicides have reduced the need to hoe.

Hogsheads are very large wooden barrels and the word refers to volume. Hogsheads were used in colonial times to transport and store tobacco. A standardized hogshead measured forty-eight inches long and thirty inches in diameter. When filled with tobacco, a hogshead would weigh about a thousand pounds. They were usually rolled to a nearby river, where they were loaded onto flatboats and shipped to markets in larger ports.

House burn is the damage incurred by tobacco leaves from too much moisture, which allows mold and bacteria to grow. This generally occurs when there is too much rain and the fires have not been hot enough or weren't started soon enough. House burn can also indicate that tobacco was hung too close together in the barn. Tobacco with house burn is less valuable.

In order is the western Kentucky vernacular equivalent to the term *in case* used in other parts of the state. The phrase means that the tobacco has just the right amount of moisture and is ready for stripping, prizing, and sending onto market.

Jackson Purchase is the land located between the Tennessee and Mississippi Rivers in the far western region of Kentucky. President Andrew Jackson bought the land from the Chickasaw Indians in 1818.

Loose-leaf warehouse refers to facilities where tobacco is sold at public auction.

Lugs are the leaves found at the base of the tobacco plant. They are generally smaller in size and thickness and bring less money when sold.

Moist snuff tobacco is a type of smokeless tobacco, consumed by placing a small amount of cut leaves between the cheek and gum or upper lip. Remaining juices may be spit into a nearby container.

Oiling tobacco is the process used to treat each tobacco plant with a chemical to inhibit the growth of suckers.

Pool tobacco refers to tobacco that did not meet the government grade price point. If the buyers did not want the tobacco at the price assigned by grade, then the tobacco was assigned to the pool. The association then took the tobacco to their warehouse, packed it in a hogshead, and kept it until they could find a buyer. The farmer was paid the same day that his other tobacco was sold at the warehouse.

Price support for tobacco occurred from 1938 until 2004. The federal government regulated the production of tobacco by establishing acreage allotments and marketing quotas. In order to guarantee the farmer a fair price, the US Department of Agriculture set the support price to be paid for tobacco using a formula. If the farmer did not get the support price when he sold his tobacco, he would still be paid the support price with a loan from the government.

Prizing tobacco means to compress the cured tobacco leaves into a container called a hogshead. Prizing was usually accomplished with a handheld device that applied pressure and was operated by a farm or warehouse worker.

Quota refers to the amount of tobacco the federal government will allow a farmer to grow and sell. If a farmer produces more than their quota, they must either destroy the excess, sell it at a penalty, or store it until the following year, selling it against that year's quota.

Scorched tobacco describes tobacco that has had too high a temperature or heat during the curing process.

Setting tobacco refers to the placement of each slip of tobacco into the ground. Before modern advances in technology, each plant was hand pegged into the soil. Since the 1940s, mechanized tobacco setters have made the process much less laborious.

Side dressing is fertilizing the soil alongside each row to enhance the growth of tobacco plants.

Snuff is ground, cured, and flavored tobacco. It is generally used by taking a small pinch between the thumb and forefinger, and sniffed into the nostril.

Spiking means to spear the stalk of a tobacco plant onto a tobacco stick. Once the stick is filled with five or six tobacco plants, it is hung in a barn to cure.

Stripping was the process of pulling the tobacco leaves off the stalks by hand. The color and thickness of the leaves determined their category—prime or lugs. The process required the stripper to know good leaves from the not-so-good. The process is much easier now as all leaves are packed into containers for market.

Suckers are the flowering buds that come out at each leaf where it connects to the stalk. Each time suckers are removed, another bud will begin to form if the plant is not treated.

Suckering tobacco means to remove suckers (flowering buds), which appear as new growth after tobacco is topped. There is a sucker behind every leaf and occasionally, a plant will have two suckers that must be removed. At one time, suckers were removed by hand, but in modern tobacco farming, chemical compounds are used and the process is called oiling tobacco.

Sweated tobacco refers to the fermentation process of curing tobacco when the nitrates and tannins are removed and the color is set. If a tobacco is sweated, it has lost body and the price is greatly reduced at market.

The Trust was a consortium of East Coast tobacco manufacturers organized into the American Tobacco Company; it was organized in 1890 by James B. Duke, president of W. Duke and Sons. The consortium was made up of five enterprises: W. Duke and Sons, Kinney Tobacco Company, Allen and Ginter, William S. Kimball, and Goodwin and Company. By 1901, the American Tobacco Company had become international. A deal was struck with the British Imperial Tobacco Company to limit competition. Soon, the Italian Regie Tobacco Company had an agreement, as well. Within twenty years, the Trust had bought out more than 250 of its competitors and controlled the price paid to farmers for tobacco.

Tobacco buyout is the term commonly used to mean the Fair and Equitable Tobacco Reform Act (FETRA), which became Title VII of the American Jobs Creation Act of 2004. The buyout is federal legislation enacted to significantly change US tobacco policy. The act repealed the federal tobacco price support and quota programs, and disposed of existing pool stocks. It also paid tobacco quota owners and growers for their quotas. The buyout was set over a ten-year period, with payments ending in 2014.

Tobacco knives were used during harvest to split the stalk, then cut the tobacco close to the ground. The handle was generally made of wood and the blade of sharpened steel. Tobacco knives used at Smith Farms resemble a tomahawk.

Tobacco markets: in early America, farmers packed or *prized* their tobacco into a wooden hogshead, made by a cooper. These large, round casks were held together with staves and tobacco leaves were layered inside. Men would use a hand press to compress the tobacco to almost a solid mass, then roll the cask to the river for shipping to larger ports. Modern transportation has led from the river, to rail, and eventually to highways. In the past two hundred years, a western Kentucky farmer would typically take his crop to a local warehouse, where buyers for manufacturers would place bids on the crops. Often, the tobacco would be sent to markets in Hopkinsville or Louisville. An alternative method was to sell the crop directly to buyers from the farmer's own barn. Since the tobacco buyout of 2004, the tobacco companies tell farmers how much to grow, the farmer grows it, and sells it directly to the tobacco companies.

Tobacco notes refers to legal tender for public money, serving as commercial paper. Tobacco notes were used in exchange for other commodities or in payment of debts.

Tobacco sticks are made of wood, approximately four feet in length and one inch in diameter, and are used to hang tobacco leaves in the barn for curing.

Tobacco warehouses are facilities where tobacco is sold at public auction for sixty to ninety days each season.

Tobacco worms are pesky green worms that eat the foliage of the tobacco plant. Before the widespread use of chemicals, worms were removed by hand.

Topping refers to the labor-intensive process of breaking off the flowers of each plant before any flowers open to encourage the leaves to ripen. Topping may need to be done more than once to have the best effect.

Warehouse auctioning systems evolved around 1860 and were established in order to sell tobacco at a public sale, where it was sold to the highest bidder. The owner of the tobacco was offered the right to reject the bids and if the bids were not rejected, the tobacco was delivered to the purchaser at the warehouse.

References

W. F. Axton, *Tobacco and Kentucky* (Lexington, KY: University Press of Kentucky, 1975).

Bobbie Smith Bryant, *Forty Acres and a Red Belly Ford: The Smith Family of Calloway County* (Lexington, KY: Clark Publishing, 2011).

Effie Marquess Carmack, *Out of the Black Patch: The Autobiography of Effie Marquess Carmack* (Logan, UT: Utah State University Press, 1999).

Tracy Campbell, *Politics of Despair* (Lexington, KY: University Press of Kentucky, 1993).

Thomas D. Clark, *A History of Kentuc*ky (Ashland, KY: The Jesse Stuart Foundation, 1988).

Thomas D. Clark, *Agrarian Kentucky* (Lexington, KY: University Press of Kentucky, 1977).

Thomas D. Clark, Lowell H. Harrison, and James C. Klotter, *The Kentucky Encyclopedia* (Lexington, KY: University Press of Kentucky, 1992).

William Elsey Connelley and Dr. E. M. Coulter, *History of Kentucky* (Chicago, IL: The American Historical Society, 1922).

Bill Cunningham, *On Bended Knees: the Night Rider Story* (Nashville, TN: McClanahan Publishing House, 1983).

Jeffery A. Duvall, "Knowing About the Tobacco: Women, Burley, and Farming in the Central Ohio River Valley," *Register of the Kentucky Historical Society* (Autumn 2010): 108, no. 4.

Lowell H. Harrison and Dr. James C. Klotter, *A New History of Kentucky* (Lexington, KY: University Press of Kentucky, 1997).

Dorothy and Kerby Jennings, *The Story of Calloway County 1822-1976* (Murray, KY: Murray Democrat Publishing Co., 1980).

James O. Nall, *The Tobacco Night Riders of Kentucky and Tennessee* (Kuttawa, KY: McClanahan Publishing House, 1991).

Patty Rantf, "Preserving the Black Patch Heritage," *Kentucky Monthly Magazine* (November 2012): 6.

Kelly Tiller, Will Snell, and Blake Brown, *Tobacco Quota Buyout: Questions and Answers* (Lexington, KY: University of Kentucky Cooperative Extension, University of Kentucky College of Agriculture, 2004).

Richard Ulack, Karl Raitz, and Gyula Paue, *Atlas of Kentucky* (Lexington, KY: University Press of Kentucky, 1998).

Hambleton Tapp and James C. Klotter, *Kentucky: Decades of Discord 1865-1900* (Frankfort, KY: Kentucky Historical Society, 1977).

John Van Willigen and Susan C. Eastwood, *Tobacco Culture: Farming Kentucky's Burley Belt* (Lexington, KY: University Press of Kentucky, 1998).

(Betsy Bryant)

About the Author

Bobbie Smith Bryant is a native of Murray, Kentucky, in the Jackson Purchase region of Western Kentucky. Bobbie grew up on her family's tobacco farm. She now draws upon that background for her writing projects. She is proud of her family's ten-generation farming heritage and today provides marketing and promotional assistance, as well as historic and genealogical research about Smith Farms.

Bobbie lives in Jefferson County with her husband and best friend, Bill. She serves the Kentucky League of Cities as a community development advisor. For more than twenty years she has assisted Kentucky cities with community and economic development issues. Bobbie is a professional facilitator and also instructs community leaders on a multitude of topics.

Through her career path she has honed her skills in a variety of venues. At one time she owned and managed a successful retail business. She also hosted a daily morning television show and a monthly broadcast featuring notable people of western Kentucky.

In 2010, Bobbie and her family published *Forty Acres and a Red Belly Ford: The Smith Family of Calloway County.* In this book, the time honored tradition of farming and life on the farm are shared through the retelling of family stories, photographs, and shared memories.

Her second book was published in 2013 and is titled *Passions of the Black Patch: Cooking and Quilting in Western Kentucky.* It features over 200 regional recipes, a collection of colorful handcrafted quilts, and delightful short stories from one of the commonwealth's unique areas.

Bobbie also served as associate producer of *Farming in the Black Patch*, a PBS documentary produced by Michael Breeding Media, which continues to air on KET. The film traces the arduous task of running and operating a modern tobacco farm.

Bobbie Bryant (Photo courtesy of Ulysses Hayes, Kentucky League of Cities.)

In addition to writing, Bobbie is a featured speaker of the Kentucky Humanities Council.

Index

T

U

V

W

Z